NANTUCKET DOORWAYS:

Thresholds to the Past

by Edouard A. Stackpole
and Melvin B. Summerfield

MADISON BOOKS
Lanham • New York • London

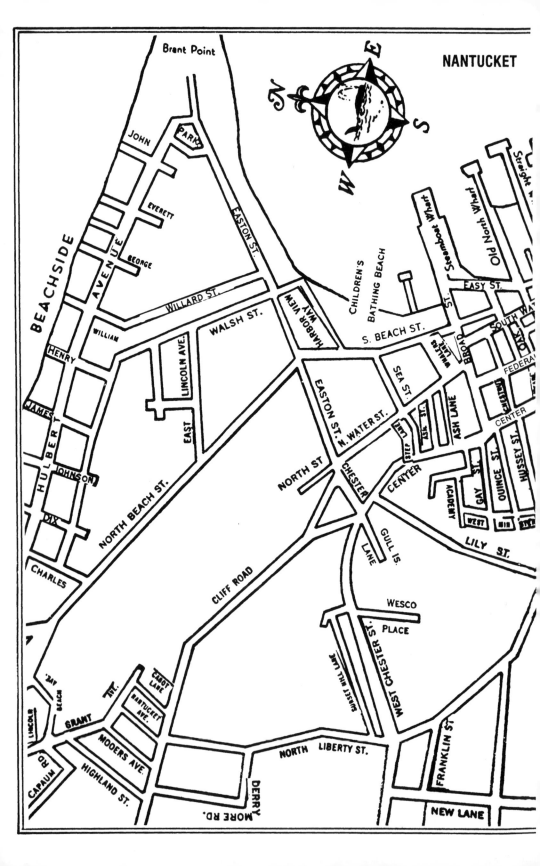

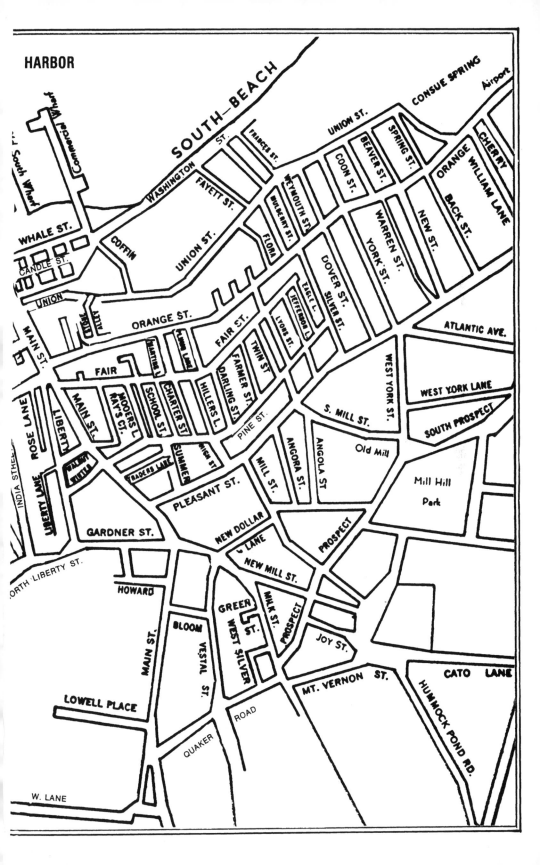

Madison Books edition published 1992.

Published by Madison Books
4501 Forbes Boulevard, Suite 200
Lanham, Maryland 20706

Distributed by National Book Network

The paper used in this publication meets the minimum
requirements of American National Standard for
Information Sciences-Permanence of Paper for Printed
Library Materials, ANSI Z39.48-1984.

Library of Congress Cataloging-in-Publication Data

Stackpole, Edouard A., 1905-
Nantucket doorways : thresholds to the past I Edouard A.
Stackpole and Melvin B. Summerfield.
p.   cm.
Originally published: New York : Hastings House, 1974.
Includes index.
1. Doorways-Massachusetts-Nantucket.
I. Summerfield, Melvin B.   II. Title.
[NA3010.S7   1992]
720'.9744'97-dc20   92-11136 CIP

ISBN: 978-0-8191-8660-7

British Cataloging in Publication Information Available

CONTENTS/ILLUSTRATIONS

NANTUCKET DOORWAYS

IN ITS far-flung position out in the Atlantic, off the coast of New England, the island of Nantucket is known today is a famed summer resort. Like a jewel in its insular setting, the town of Nantucket is the best preserved seaport in America, being the only existing community of the seventeenth and eighteenth centuries remaining very nearly intact in its original location. Nestled about its excellent harbor, the old shingled dwellings and clap-boarded mansions lining the town's winding streets and lanes reflect the spirit of the past. Surrounded by the gently rolling heathland, green pine groves and blue-water ponds, the old town has the island itself to serve as a setting for its architectural jewels.

This unique island-town is not only a valued part of America's maritime history; it serves as a representative of international history as well. From 1730 to 1830 Nantucket was the leading port in the pursuit of an industry known as the Southern Whale Fishery. This was a new marine enterprise which the island whalemen not only created but developed. Three factors made this possible: the self reliance which marked the first settlers; the coming of the Quaker religion to the island community; and the pioneering spirit of the original whalemen. As the eighteenth century developed, the adventurous mariners built up a fleet of nearly a hundred whaleships; the shore-side industries of the sail-loft, ropewalk, cooper shop, oil refinery, and candle house became economic successes; the coastwise and trans-Atlantic vessels, bringing oil and candles to the marketplaces of Boston, Philadelphia, Baltimore, and Charleston, as well as to London, Lisbon, and Amsterdam, brought return cargoes to enrich the island community.

Competition from newly established whaling ports on the mainland, notably New Bedford; the physical handicap of shoals across the harbor mouth; two devastating fires which destroyed the waterfront and business sections of the town; the gold rush to California; discovery of "rock oil" in Pennsylvania; and the Civil War—all were successive economic disasters which brought to an end Nantucket's sole industry—whaling. Just over a century ago her last whaleship was sold in a foreign port and the island's maritime days of glory were at an end.

During the declining years the old town gradually fell asleep. A few efforts were made to establish an industry to replace whaling, but all failed for one reason or another. Depression descended like a cloud over the town. Houses fell into disrepair; fences toppled into yards; grass grew up through the cobbled streets and along the lanes; an air of melancholy blended with the atmosphere of an island community that had virtually abandoned itself to an accepted fate.

But Nantucket did not become a ghost town. A new way of life came into being—a new business developed—that of a type called "summer business." Beginning with the 1870's the town and island gradually became a favored summer home for people from the mainland who appreciated the quiet charm and recreational opportunities that Nantucket provided. Aside from the excellent climate, sea bathing, sailing, outdoor sporting activities, and serenity, there was another factor that attracted the visitor. The ancient character of the town.

Nantucket had experienced its depression at a time when the rest of New England was enjoying a period of new building. Because it was necessary that the islanders preserve their dwellings, they escaped the general rebuilding boom and as a result, the ancient structures were repaired and retained and many who came as visitors purchased old houses and restored them. Gradually an appreciation for the spirit of the island's unique traditions began to govern the life of the entire community; this culminated with the town's designation as an "Historic District," which continues to protect Nantucket from modern innovations.

In this approach to the history of Nantucket there is an opportunity to combine the visible scene with both the artistic values of the town's architectural appeal and the intangibles of the human spirit of this maritime community. Here is a town in the sea, literally created by the elemental forces of geographical separation from the mainland, developed by a daring industry— whaling—and expanded under the guidance of a religious sect —the Quakers.

A great philosopher once noted:
> The artistic representation of history is a more serious pursuit than the exact writing of history. For the art of letters goes to the heart of things, whereas the factual report merely collocates details.

How fortunate we are to have the town of Nantucket as a community where the physical aspects of an historic past have been so carefully preserved. Whaling, one of the most adventuresome industries, built this town, and the homes of the mariners who cruised through all the oceans of the world and of the craftsmen who fitted out the ships are symbolic of the seafaring traditions they created. Here also are the humble dwellings of the workmen who refined the oil and molded the spermaceti candles, of the merchants and ship owners who sent these products to Europe and America to provide light for the homes, manor houses, palaces, and streets of towns and cities.

This atmosphere of the past—this flavor so redolent of the sea—has provided Nantucket with its basic appeal. Altogether, the town has become a legacy to this nation, a living reminder of a fine maritime tradition created by a self-reliant, sturdy people.

To walk along the streets and lanes is in itself an excursion through the byways of our national history. No insular community this—rather a seaport which was known in the eighteenth century as the headquarters of an important new industry: the Southern Whale Fishery.

It is this intangible blending of past and present which makes a visit to Nantucket such a memorable experience. Such harmonious blending conveys a close and warm association with tradition. While we cannot, of course, touch this or any tradition in the visible sense, we soon become aware of it because of the very presence of the town. We may become interpreters as we stroll up cobbled Main Street, or follow a narrow side street, or walk along the very outskirts of the town's perimeter. The houses, large or small, humble dwelling or impressive mansion, provide a medium through which we may call up the lives of the people who created and developed this seaport town.

Such a study is an exciting venture into the past. It involves an opportunity to learn of a people by allowing the physical evidences of the town to serve as an introduction to the stimulating details. And as we become more aware of the owners of these houses something of their personalities is established; we may use even this slender knowledge as a satisfying bridge between the town's past and present.

Having thus adopted the role of the student, we are no longer the casual observer. This enables us to follow a pleasant procedure. We will figuratively approach the house, mount the steps, and apply the brass knocker gently against the door, then pause, waiting for the door to swing open. Soon we will feel the presence of the owner of the house. We do not, of course, expect to see anyone. Then, in as quiet a manner as possible, we ask: "Is Captain Macy at home? I would like to speak to him." Or, at another doorway, say: "Miss Starbuck wished me to call this morning." And, at yet another door: "Mr. Swain expects me at two o'clock. I am perhaps early, but would appreciate seeing him."

Thus, we have this study to serve as the intermediary—as a means of introduction. If we are to test the sincerity of its purpose we must be willing listeners to the story which is forthcoming. In most cases, more than a century has elapsed since the original families lived within, but the present-day owners have cared for these old homes and have restored them with both an understanding of the past and a concept of today's world. Once we knock at these doors with a true desire to learn there will be an immeasurably satisfying answer.

The New England poet Longfellow conveyed so well the traditional aspects of our seaport towns; one of his verses may be particularly associated with Nantucket:

> Old houses wherein men have lived and died,
> Are haunted houses. Through the open doors,
> The harmless phantoms on their errands glide
> With feet that make no noise upon the floor.

In these streets and homes we may meet such figures of the past. We may find them in the humble dwelling of the foremast hand; in the domicile of the rigger, cooper, or sailmaker; in the snug home of the coasting skipper or mate; in the "four-square" residence of the shipmaster; or in the imposing mansion of the ship owner and merchant. And all these houses are within the range of the stroller.

There could be no more favorable place for our walk through the town to begin than at Main Street's cobbled square. Here is an old-world marketplace, for two centuries the heart of the business life of the seaport. Brick stores, built soon after the Great Fire of 1846, make fitting bulwarks along the north side and companion brick structures balance the scene where Orange Street merges into Main.

The Pacific National Bank, erected in 1818, fourteen years after it was founded, heads the square. Here stone steps, flanked by iron railings, lead to the door crowned with a fanlight, under a semi-circular portico with two Ionic columns. A center of the financial activities in Nantucket since its founding, the bank has witnessed a remarkable array of both islanders and "summer people" entering and leaving through this doorway, including shipmasters, Quaker elders, lady shopkeepers, ship owners, schoolteachers, clerks, statesmen, ministers, merchants, politicians, sailors, town officials, Presidents of the United States, foreign dignitaries, and thrifty schoolboys.

Among those who served the bank faithfully was William Mitchell. During his years as cashier (1837 to 1861) he lived with his family in the chambers above the banking rooms. Beginning his career as a schoolteacher, William Mitchell's life was a veritable quest for knowledge; he became a recognized astronomer and scientist and was elected a Fellow of Harvard College. It was on the roof of the Pacific National Bank that this remarkable Nantucketer built a small observatory, and his daughter Maria (also his outstanding pupil), became his assistant, regularly scanning the night skies with her father's telescope.

One evening in October, 1847, while sweeping the heavens with the brass telescope, Maria Mitchell saw a strange white object in the lens—an almost ethereal body. She called her father, who duly recorded the fact. Several months elapsed before the scientists of the world acknowledged that Miss Mitchell, of Nantucket, was the first astronomer to have discovered a comet. World fame followed. She became the first woman voted into the American Academy of Arts and Sciences and the King of Denmark had a gold medal especially struck off for her. She left her position as Librarian at the Atheneum following her appointment as the first Professor of Astronomy at Vassar College.

Many of the island's distinguished visitors enjoyed an opportunity to go "up scuttle" to William Mitchell's rooftop observatory. One of these, Ralph Waldo Emerson, who had come to Nantucket for a lecture, wrote: "In William Mitchell's observa-

The Pacific National Bank. Main Street.

tory I saw the nebula in Cassiopea . . ." On his first visit to Nantucket in 1852, Herman Melville noted: "We passed the evening with Mr. Mitchell and his celebrated daughter, the discoverer of comets."

On the steps in front of this door a variety of tableaux might have been recorded as people stopped for a moment's chat. We might now see President Grant being escorted by Frederick C. Sanford, the bank's president; Charles O'Conor, first Catholic ever nominated for the Presidency, removing his hat as he greets Miss Gulielma Folger; Breckinridge Long, Ambassador to Italy, acknowledging in his courtly way the "good morning" of an islander; David Sarnoff, decades before he became leader of the giant corporation RCA, entering to deposit in his savings account a portion of his salary as an operator for the Marconi Wireless Station at Siasconset; Eastman Johnson, extraordinary portrait painter, looking with a practiced eye at the faces of the towns-people, many of whom he immortalized on his canvases in anonymity; Captain George Pollard, ill-fated master of the whale-ship *Essex,* which was sunk by a whale, enroute to quietly cash his check as a night watchman, carefully avoiding casual conversation with passersby; Colonel Robert Stewart, who as a Rough Rider had ridden up San Juan Hill with Teddy Roosevelt; and Regis Post, first Governor-General of the newly acquired territory of Puerto Rico.

William Mitchell himself, in his quiet way, always liked to recall that inimitable wag, Captain Joseph Clapp, who one morning opened the door and called across the banking room, "William, have you got any of those Bank of Jerusalem bonds? I hear they'll yield twenty percent—if you get inside the pearly gates!"

William Mitchell, that remarkable teacher-scientist-cashier, occupied the bank's upper chambers until his wife's death in 1861, when he retired from the old familiar scene. If anyone ever entered the "pearly gates" it was this man—the outstanding Nantucketer of the island's nineteenth century.

Turning into Liberty Street from the bank, we come to the first house to the right, next to the Methodist Church. Liberty

Benjamin Barney House. 1 Liberty Street.

Street is one of the oldest of the town's thoroughfares, having been originally a section of that early division of house-lot land known as the Wesco Acre Lots. No. 1 was built in the 1720's for Benjamin Barney, who had come from Newport, Rhode Island, to marry Lydia Starbuck of Nantucket. The marriage took place in 1726, and it is probable the house was built shortly thereafter. Two chimneys at the ridge pole gave the little house a strong appearance, which the basic construction bears out. The front doorway, with its transom, is in excellent proportion to the front windows, two on either hand, with small-paned sash. Benjamin and Lydia were the parents of eight children. When in 1758 the fourth daughter of the family, Elizabeth Barney, married young William Rotch, the house assumed a role in maritime history; Rotch became one of the outstanding whaling merchants in the international world. We may visualize the courtship of this Quaker couple, witnessed by this doorway, as the tall, serious-minded William escorted Elizabeth home from Quaker meetings and lingered on the doorstep.

In those days the island was on the threshold of its burgeoning period as the greatest of the whaling ports, the pioneer of a new industry known as the Southern Whale Fishery. William Rotch was to become the greatest whaling merchant of his time— a man who would challenge the right of any single nation to control the industry; a man who would propose the establishment of a Nantucket whaling colony in England and, because of political indecision on the part of the King's ministers, would successfully transfer the project to France; a man who would face the economic challenges of powerful London firms as well as endure the criticism of his fellow merchants in Nantucket; a man whose influence would have much to do with shaping the destiny of the future city of New Bedford.

Liberty Street, as one leaves the Pacific Bank corner, has a gentle slope upward before dipping to the west and beginning its meandering way to North Liberty Street. Laid out in 1678 along the southern boundary of the Wesco Acre Lots, it is a street with many historic houses in island chronicles. As we follow it we may relive the stories of several and discover much of the larger history of the town as well.

There is a definite atmosphere about the doorway at No. 5 Liberty Street. While the house, with its great central chimney, its roof walk, and wide front, is not unlike others of the 1740 period when Barnabas Pinkham built it, there is a quality of dignity as well as age here. The brownstone step, with iron

Paul West House. 5 Liberty Street.

scrapers for muddy boots; the paneled door with pilasters; the small-paned window sash—all belong to the solid character of the period in which Nantucket prospered.

The nameplate on the door bears a name in simple letters: "Paul West." It is a brief identification, terse and clear, as was the personality of the man who put it there. Paul West was a particularly successful whaling master. He began his career as a ship's boy at the age of thirteen when he sailed from Nantucket on William Rotch's favorite whaleship, the *Maria*. His rise through the ranks of the whaleship officers was steady and in 1803 he was selected as master of the whaleship *Cyrus,* which was one of Rotch's ships out of Dunkirk that was captured by the British and taken to London. After twenty years at sea, Paul West returned home to retire with a competency at the age of thirty-nine.

How he made his fortune became a controversial question among his descendants. He actually established his reputation as a dependable mariner while serving as mate on ships sailing from the port of Dunkirk, France, where the fleet of Nantucket whaleships led by William Rotch had established a whaling port. When the British captured one of these vessels, the *Cyrus,* Paul West accepted an offer by the new owner, a London merchant, to be her master. After two successful voyages around Cape Horn, Captain West was given command of a new ship, the *Charlton,* and again returned with a full ship. These voyages were made at the time of the Napoleonic Wars, and Captain West sailed in armed whaleships, also holding commissions as "letter-of-marque," or privateer. At the outbreak of the War of 1812, Captain West brought his ship safely back to London, but, rather than becoming involved in a conflict involving his homeland, he returned to Nantucket with his wife, the former Phoebe Hussey, daughter of Captain Benjamin Hussey and a Nantucketer, who he had married in Dunkirk.

Paul West, master mariner, was only thirty-nine years old when he came home, but he had acquired a sizable fortune. He had been twenty years a whaleman, but the question arose: Did he acquire his competency by whaling or by privateering? A century after his retirement (in 1916) two of his descendants took opposite sides in the family debate. It all probably would have amused the venerable captain, who lived in happy retirement for fifty years in his island home. A contemporary wrote of him in his passing: "Captain West was a model shipmaster, methodical and exact in his habits and care of his ship. His house and grounds reflected the very patterns of orderliness that characterized his life."

No doubt the good captain's handling of his investments had as much to do with his business success as the handling of his ships had to do with his reputation as a successful mariner. To retire at the age of thirty-nine was an accomplishment in itself, but to then enjoy a half-century with his family in his native town was an even more satisfying experience.

Continuing our stroll through Nantucket's maritime history we pass a house (No. 9) that was moved to the site for Captain Edward Joy in 1841. Among the vessels commanded by him were the *Lydia* and the *Constitution*. The house next door was built in the 1740's for Thomas and William Starbuck, who conveyed it to their sister, the wife of Silvanus Allen. Across the way, at the corner of Walnut Lane, is the Nathaniel Macy House, which goes back to the early history of the first homestead lands at old Sherborn—the original name of Nantucket Town. Tradition has it that it was moved to Liberty Street around 1740, and that it may have been the home of Thomas Macy, one of the first group of settlers, who built it originally near Wannacomet Pond. Of a lean-to design, it was carefully restored in the 1930's by the Rev. George P. Christian and in 1970 presented to the Nantucket Historical Association by Mrs. Christian. It is open to the public during the summer season.

The double-step stoop serves as a perfect setting for the front door, with its transom and wide panels. A quarter-century ago, when the house was being restored, the original door, together with the side framing, was found in the attic, and both were promptly restored. In working on the great fireplaces on the first floor, two small "built-in" fireplaces were removed before the original was uncovered in both kitchen and keeping room.

Nathaniel Macy House. 12 Liberty Street.

The simple lines of this dwelling provide a perfect picture of the style favored by the first settlers, a style which traditionally served for houses both in old and new Sherborn in the eighteenth century. So strongly constructed were these homes that to move them from their sites to the new town was practical indeed, for almost all the dimensional timber for house-building was brought to Nantucket from New Hampshire and Maine. The Christian House is one of a dozen or more still standing that was moved in from the old homestead area west of the present town.

The Macy family owned both sides of Walnut Lane, and Nathaniel Macy received this house-lot in 1741, when the house was moved here. In its original location it probably faced the south, as did its fellows, but like so many of the town houses, it was placed in the most convenient position along the street line. Historians place its date of first erection in 1720. Thus, we have a house which has lived through two and a half centuries of island life and which serves as a strong reminder of the type of people who built this "unknown city in the ocean"—as Daniel Webster described Nantucket after his visit in 1828.

There are a few of the old "double houses" in the town, and 27 Liberty Street is one of the oldest. Built in 1745, it was a two-family residence from the start of the nineteenth century, when Reuben and Benjamin Fosdick, sons of the original owner, shared the structure. Two other sons, Captains Samuel and Robert Calder, had adventurous lives, the former being a captive of Algerian pirates for several years, the latter surviving the dread Dartmoor Prison experience of the War of 1812.

The entrance has an enclosed porch—called by Nantucketers a "bulkhead," after shipboard terminology—and conceals two front doors which lead to the east and west apartments. Neighbors frequently visited the Calders. One was Captain William Swain, who had commanded a number of whaleships out of England, among which was the Enderby ship *Sarah & Elizabeth*. It was aboard this vessel, in the year 1832, that Thomas Beale, a young ship's surgeon, transferred from the ship *Kent* while the ships met in the western Pacific. Beale wrote one of the whaling classics from his experience—*The Natural History of the Sperm Whale*—and, in one of the exciting descriptive passages, recounted Captain Swain's capture of a giant whale: "By the most subtle management [of the whaleboat] he contrived to get near the monster and immediately struck him with the harpoon with his own hands, and, before he had time to recover from the blow, he managed with his usual dexterity to give him two fatal wounds with the lance." Captain Swain was then in his fifty-fifth year.

In the quiet of early evening, after the supper meal, these Quaker shipmasters visited one another. The exchange of their experiences was not for boasting; many a younger man gained invaluable information from their tales. Above all was the tradition of the island's whaling years lending an aura to the scene.

In the twentieth century a Nantucket man and his wife retired to their ancestral home. Mr. and Mrs. Charles Selden spent their declining years in the west side apartment, where Mr. Selden was often called upon to comment on his experiences as the Paris and London correspondent for the New York *Times*, when he covered many events between the Versailles Treaty at the end of World War I and the Lorcano Treaty, the prelude to World War II. Although he never went to sea, he was wont to remark that the adventures of his grandfather, Captain Sylvester Hodges, were a challenge to him. On one occasion, after telling of a difficult assignment, he said: "When I thought of him sailing a seventy-foot brig from Nantucket to the Antarctic Ocean, hunting for seals in the South Shetland Islands with no charts to help him, I never considered any of the tasks which first appeared insurmountable as being impossible."

Further along, and across the street, the front steps leading to the entrance of 26 Liberty Street are a good example of the clever carpentry which makes an easier ascent for a steep rise from the sidewalk. The house, on its high brick basement, with its great center chimney, square facade, small-paned windows, and general air of strength, was the home of a remarkable whaling master: Captain Benjamin Worth. If ever a mariner left a record to be envied it was Captain Worth. The bare statistics are amazing:

During his career (1783 to 1824) he was almost continuously at sea. He sailed over 870,000 sea miles. Of his voyages, he made: one to London; four to the west coast of Africa; one to the east coast of Africa; five to the Brazil Banks; one to the West

Fosdick-Calder House. 27 Liberty Street.

Indies; one to Davis Straits; one to the northwest coast of America; five to the Pacific Ocean, on one of which, in the *Brothers,* he was the first American whaler to go to Australia.

He passed Cape Horn sixteen times and the Cape of Good Hope twice; on two voyages he circumnavigated the world. His total catch of oil was nineteen thousand barrels, of which all but four thousand barrels were sperm oil. During this time he never lost a man from a shipboard accident, and the only vessel he lost was the *George,* which was captured during the War of 1812 and sent into Halifax. Previous to this capture, however, while in the Pacific Ocean, the *George* was hailed by the American frigate *Essex,* just arrived in that ocean, and Captain David Porter obtained from Captain Worth information as to the whereabouts of the British whaleships, their descriptions, etc., which led to the ultimate destruction of the British fleet.

There was tragedy, however, following Captain Worth's retirement, when word came that his oldest son, Captain Charles Worth, had died in Valparaiso from a wound from his own lance, received while in his boat attacking a whale. The young man was then in his thirty-seventh year and was in command of the London whaler *Rochester.* Living with her husband's parents at their Liberty Street home at the time the news arrived was Captain Charles' wife, Ann Young Worth, who had met and married him in England, and who had come to Nantucket with her child in anticipation of her husband rejoining her in his island home.

On the west side of Winter Street, connecting Liberty with Main Street, stands an imposing brick building—the Coffin School. Erected in 1852, it was the second structure to house that school, the first being on Fair Street, where the school was launched in 1827. When the school's trustees decided to erect the new building they chose the geographical center of the town; the structure itself was designed in accordance with the best of the Greek Revival Period pieces, with a high limestone and granite foundation, to be a handsome brick schoolhouse.

The iron fence guarding the brick path leads to the recessed portico entrance, which is flanked by two white wooden pillars

The Coffin School. Winter Street.

of Doric style. During the nineteenth century the Coffin School continued as a private school, offering academic instruction for both boys and girls. After a half-century of affiliation with the public schools in the twentieth century, it again became a private institution, providing quarters for the town's kindergarten in the brick addition (built in 1918) and offering college and adult educational courses with the Nantucket Institute each summer.

It is the historical background of the school which gives it a special significance. It was founded by a British admiral who wished to perpetuate the memory of his Nantucket ancestor, Tristram Coffin, the progenitor of all the Coffins in America. Admiral Sir Isaac Coffin was born in Boston—whereas his father had come from Nantucket—and entered the Royal Navy before the outbreak of the Revolutionary War. In 1827, after a visit to the island, he founded the school and also purchased the brig *Clio* to serve as a seagoing adjunct. Although the latter was discontinued after a few years, the Coffin School itself continued, being endowed by the doughty admiral. At the time of the founding the old warrior, with typical humor, stipulated that only those of Coffin blood on the island would be eligible to attend. By that time practically all the inhabitants who were descendants of the first settlers could trace their ancestry back to Tristram Coffin through either his sons or daughters.

The marble steps of the school's entrance show the wear of the many footsteps of those who have attended classes over the years. But they are still sound, and solid enough for those scholars of the future who may wish to find learning therein.

Passersby on Main Street in the early 1890's may have seen a man carrying a cane make his way laboriously up the front steps of 84 Main Street, on the corner of Pine. The man was William Hussey Macy, and he was blind—stricken only a few years before at the height of his unusual career. In his youth he had been a whaleman, but later had volunteered for service in the U.S. Army in the first months of the Civil War. Wounded during the campaign before Wilmington, North Carolina, he returned home to recover and adopt a third method of making a

Coleman-Macy House. 84 Main Street.

livelihood. The change was excellent. His letters home from the war scene had attracted the attention of the editors of *The Inquirer and Mirror,* and he soon became their chief writer on things nautical. In time, he accepted the assignment to write editorials, and inaugurated a column called "Here and There," which continues to this day.

Encouraged by his readers, Macy began writing short stories for several weekly magazines, notably the *Flag of the Union* and *Ballou's,* the latter a monthly. So well received were these stories that he decided to write a book based on his own whaling experiences. Titled *Thar She Blows,* it was published in 1876, and was so popular that a second edition was printed. His work with the newspaper continued, and, upon the request of friends, he was a candidate for the post of Registrar of Deeds in the town government and won the election.

Then came two disasters that would have destroyed an ordinary man. First, his eyesight began failing at an alarming rate, and then, his wife died and he was left with a young family to maintain. Two months later total blindness overcame him. The double tragedy nearly overwhelmed him, but the courage of the man came to the fore. He designed a wooden frame which could be placed over a writing pad or book, enabling him to carry on his writing. The town, recognizing his unique talent, permitted him to carry on his office at the registry for several more years.

As a young man, on his first whaling voyage in the ship *Planter,* of Nantucket, William Hussey Macy had kept a journal. On a July day in 1842, while the ship lay at anchor in the harbor of Nukaheva in the Marquesas Islands of the South Seas, Macy recorded that five men had deserted from the ship *Acushnet,* which was moored some distance away. One of those deserters was an embryo whaleman named Herman Melville, and young Macy's entry in his journal is the only existing contemporary account of that incident—an incident leading to Melville's *Typee* —the beginning of the literary career of the man who was to write what is considered to be America's greatest classic—*Moby-Dick.*

The crossing threads of the lanes and streets weave a pattern that binds the old town of Nantucket and forms the ancient coverlet that so richly envelops the present scene. Pine Street is the western boundary of the original house-lot layout known as the Fish Lots. That portion of Pine Street leading south from Main, and curving slightly at the meeting with Mooers' Lane, was at one time known as Hayscale Lane, tradition asserting that a platform scales was placed in the narrow part of the roadway so that wagon-loads of produce and whale oil, as well as hay, could be weighed. It is known that Levi Starbuck had an oil refinery further up the street, and that the thoroughfare was a link to Main Street and thence to the wharves.

But our next stop is just around the corner at the first turn in Pine Street, into Mooers' Lane, a narrow roadway leading east toward Fair Street. During most of the nineteenth century this little passageway was known as "Judith Chase's Lane," and it is the Chase House that we will visit. Erected on this site in 1745, the chimney end being the oldest section, this ancient dwelling sits on a slight angle to the lane, giving it a strange appearance but a distinct character.

Here lived one of Nantucket's seafaring families—the Chases; two of the sons—Lieutenant Reuben Chase and Captain Joseph Chase—became outstanding mariners. On the dusk of an early evening we can imagine the homecoming of Lieutenant Reuben Chase in 1784. The Revolutionary War had been over for a year, but Reuben, of the young U.S. Navy, had left the service in 1781 to join with French-American privateers out of L'Orient. He was now home—to prepare for whaling again—after adventures enough to satisfy most men.

Soon after the first year of the war had proved to Nantucket whalemen the industry was temporarily doomed, Reuben Chase made his way to Portsmouth to join the crew of the naval ship *Ranger,* which was under the command of a dynamic leader named John Paul Jones. During the ship's voyage the tall figure of Reuben Chase (six feet, four inches) attracted the attention of Commodore Jones. Promotion was rapid for this seafaring son of Nantucket, whose ability as a mariner was matched by his cool

Chase House. 7 Mooers' Lane.

conduct during sea fights. He became Lieutenant Reuben Chase by the time the *Ranger* reached France.

When Jones took the newly named *Bon Homme Richard* into the English Channel to begin his famous cruise around the British Isles, Lieutenant Reuben Chase was one of his selected officers. But Chase was not fated to be on board the *Richard* during that memorable battle with H.M.S. *Serapis* in the North Sea. Just before the two ships engaged he had been ordered to go on board a captured merchantman with a prize crew. By the time he regained the decks of the battered *Richard* the fight was nearly over, and the *Serapis* was striking her colors.

Upon his return to Nantucket, Chase decided to enter the packet trade from New York to Europe rather than go whaling, and soon became master of a ship sailing from New York to Liverpool. On one voyage Captain Chase had a pleasant few days in conversation with one of the passengers, an American author named James Fenimore Cooper. For many years a legend has persisted in Nantucket that Cooper patterned his "Long Tom Coffin," in his famous book *The Pilot,* after Captain Reuben Chase.

Captain Joseph Chase, brother of Reuben, also entered the merchant service, making several voyages to France carrying oil and candles. He sailed a number of years for Micajah and Zenas Coffin. When the Nantucket Bank was robbed of twenty thousand dollars in species in 1796, it was Captain Chase who was delegated by the selectmen of the town to go to New York and bring back a criminal, named Weatherly, who was suspected as one of the thieves. He accomplished his mission; once the huge hands of the big Nantucket shipmaster "fastened" to the criminal he made no effort to escape. It was ironic, however, that the man eventually managed to break out of the town "gaol" some weeks later and escaped after stealing a boat from Great Point Lighthouse and sailing across to Cape Cod.

Deborah Chase, a sister of Reuben and Joseph, was of similar physical build and strength. It is recorded that on one occasion during the Revolution, when a company of Tory Refugees invaded the island, Deborah went to one of the community pumps with two pails for water, but a refugee, placed near the pump as a sentry, blocked her way. Swinging one of the buckets, she knocked the surprised man senseless, then filled the buckets and returned home.

Over the two centuries and a quarter of its existence, the house has had but five owners. The old dwelling has the look of great age, with its cluster chimney, old roof lines, and various ells. The fact that it is located aslant to the lane proves that it has remained in its original location, because, as first laid out, a wide space was at the intersection of the lanes and a narrow cartway followed straight out of Pine Street (instead of turning down Hayscale Lane) and connected with Ray's Court, thus creating a triangle at the intersections.

Proceeding along Pine Street for a few feet beyond Mooers' Lane, the pedestrian finds a little house with a gambrel roof— No. 8—which stands at the corner of another passway known as Lucretia Mott Lane. Nestled snuggly at the junction, this tiny house has a definite dignity of line which adds to its obvious charm. It is known that in the year 1750 it was left to Grafton Gardner by his father. George Gardner, namesake of the first owner, was killed at sea when a block fell from aloft and struck him on the head. The accident occurred in 1785, and a few years later the house was bought by Paul Pinkham, another mariner.

In observing the front door we notice its ideal proportions as the center entranceway, with its transom and shallow panels. In the year 1790 the new owner of the house, Captain Paul Pinkham, would have filled the entire doorway as he emerged from the dwelling; he was a big man with the traditional Pinkham breadth of chest. In 1785 he had been appointed Keeper of the Nantucket Lighthouse, newly built on the end of Great Point. It was from the tower of the Light that he made numerous surveys for his new chart, "Chart of Nantucket Shoals," which was published by Norman in Boston in 1791. Not only did it delineate the shoals around Nantucket and in the adjacent Sound, but it included Martha's Vineyard and Vineyard Sound as well as the southern shore of Cape Cod from Chatham to Falmouth. Captain Pinkham was a highly respected pilot of these waters, and his

Paul Pinkham House. 8 Pine Street.

chart was a valuable and needed contribution to local mariners; printed on the chart was a carefully worded testimonial signed by some of the leading ship owners and mariners of Nantucket.

Thus, in the smallest of homes there was created one of the largest of contributions to the nautical knowledge of the times concerning this part of the coast. For Nantucket Sound was a major portion of that watery highway connecting New England with the entire coastline of this country.

Next door on Pine Street stands a large house at the corner of School Street—No. 10. Looming large among its fellows, it assumes an even larger shape in the annals of Nantucket's history. In the big square room on the north side of the now double dwelling the first meetings of the Nantucket Society of Friends were held. The house then stood to the west of the present town at a place near the north head of Hummock Pond, having been erected in 1676 as the home of Nathaniel and Mary Starbuck.

Nantucket was then a settlement of scattered homesteads, having existed only seventeen years. Within the next century most of its inhabitants adopted the religion of the Quakers and the island became the stronghold of that sect in New England. In 1698, Thomas Chalkley, a prominent Friend, visited Nantucket and was cordially received. Another English traveling Friend, John Richardson, came to the island in 1701 and was impressed with Mary Starbuck and her influence among the inhabitants. When Thomas Story, an able member of the society, visited here in 1704 he was invited to the Starbuck house for a meeting. As a result the Nantucket Monthly Meeting of Friends was established in 1708 and the influence of the Quakers soon became dominant on the island.

With the erection of houses about the shore of the main harbor a number of the homestead dwellings in the original settlement were moved into the new area. This brought about a variety of interesting facts concerning the re-erection and re-building. The town was then called Sherborn, not becoming Nantucket until 1795, when the name of the island became the name of the county and the town.

Parliament House. 10 Pine Street.

In 1820 a Quaker carpenter named John Folger bought the Starbuck homestead and moved it to town, placing it in its present location and adding a section, now the south end. Over the years other additions enlarged the rear portions; the dwelling became a double house. Among its later owners were James Austin, a Quaker merchant, and Mary E. Crosby, the granddaughter of the whaling merchant Matthew Crosby.

No. 10 Pine Street came to be known as Parliament House, a name fully in keeping with its tradition both as a meeting place for the town fathers and as the place of origin of the Nantucket Monthly Meeting of Friends. But the sturdy wooden structure has another claim to fame: Nathaniel Starbuck became the leading whaling merchant of the early eighteenth century and one of the men who pioneered in the creation of a new and crucially important new colonial industry—deep sea whaling. It was this "business on the great water" that the Nantucketers founded and which was to eventually transform the quiet harbor into the greatest whaling port in the world.

The early settlers never dreamed of such unexpected changes, but it was their children and their children's children who were to create the phenomenal success that marked Nantucket's development from a farming community into an outstanding seaport. Nathaniel Starbuck and his associates opened their minds and hearts to Quakerism. Their faith in themselves as inaugurators of a new maritime industry must have been nurtured by the philosophy and example of the religious principles of Quakerism.

Thus, we may pause before Parliament House and note in its simple architectural lines a sturdiness of character so well exemplified by Mary and Nathaniel Starbuck and their fellow islanders.

Of Mary Starbuck, the visiting Quaker John Richardson said: "I knew at once upon seeing her that she was a great woman." That the home in which she welcomed both the advocates and the followers of Quakerism did not disappear into the mist of history, but was reestablished and given new life, seems a fitting memorial for both Nathaniel and Mary Starbuck.

Zenas Coffin House. 9 Pine Street.

Directly opposite Parliament House, on the corner of Summer Street, is the two and a half-story dwelling built in 1810 for Zenas Coffin, one of the most successful of Nantucket's eighteenth-century whaling merchants. A son of Micajah Coffin, he inherited his father's thrifty habits, serving his apprenticeship as a whaler until he commanded his own ship, the *Lydia,* and then, by shrewd investment, becoming the major owner in a fleet of whaleships. His sons, Charles G. and Henry Coffin, succeeded Zenas in the firm and named one of their ships for their enterprising father.

As an example of the enterprise of Zenas Coffin, an entry from his diary for August 1, 1801, follows:

The forenoon weather cleared. The carpenter caulking *Lydia*'s decks and others a-fitting the standard knees between the decks of the *John Jay*. Bought at vendue [auction] six bbls. rye flour, three of which we took to Benj. Walcott, the baker. . . . Took out ship *Lydia*'s pumps and sent to Paul Coffin, blockmaker. After dinner, myself, Gilbert, and Paul went up into the fields, plowed and hilled one piece of the corn . . . also, our company went and plowed and hoed among the other piece of corn. . . . (Aug. 6): Carpenters and caulkers at work putting on the trussel trees on the foremast and set up the foremast a little before sun setting. . . . Bought three-fourths of a cord of wood, carted it alongside ship *Lydia;* brought water for her casks . . . bought twenty-eight pounds of oakum from Daniel Pinkham for caulking the *John Jay*.

No task was too menial for these practical men, especially when it concerned the outfitting of their ships. A whaleship was bound on a voyage of from two to three years; most of the time was spent in the open sea. A well-found ship was a guarantee for a good voyage. Zenas Coffin, following the example of his father Micajah, established certain standards for business practice which were carefully emulated by his two sons, Charles and Henry. When Zenas died in 1828 he left the largest single fortune that had been processed through the Probate Court of Nantucket up to that time. His sons carried on the firm until the end of the Civil War, which also marked the final chapter in Nantucket's whaling business.

Leading up to the front door is a double step. Perhaps the energetic Captain Zenas wanted it that way, that he might leave home heading immediately in the right direction as soon as he had closed the door behind him.

Turning the corner into Summer Street we come to the head of a little passageway leading to Main Street known as Trader's Lane. A large house, crowned with a walk, commands our atten-

Peleg Bunker House. Trader's Lane.

tion. Here lived Captain Peleg Bunker, a mariner whose life was in direct contrast to that of Captain Zenas Coffin. Here, the doorway has a quiet Quaker serenity, with the curving fence rail adding a graceful touch to its entranceway, with a transom over the door. The four-bayed facade and windows with their twelve- over twelve-inch panes on the lower floor and nine over nine on the second floor provide dignity to a house built before the Revolution.

Captain Peleg Bunker was one of those Nantucket shipmasters who went to Dunkirk with William Rotch in 1785; he commanded the whaleships *Hope* and *Ardent* on two successful voyages out of that French port. After the French Revolution had forced the Nantucket colony of whalemen to abandon Dunkirk, Captain Bunker went to London to take command of the former Rotch ship *Falkland,* which had been captured by the British while she sailed under the French flag. Through an ironic twist of fate the *Falkland* was recaptured in the English Channel by a French privateer, and Captain Bunker and his men were treated barbarously by their captors, being marched from the coast to a prison in Verdun. The year was 1804.

During the next five years all efforts to obtain the release of Captain Bunker were rebuffed by the Napoleonic authorities in France. Finally, in 1809, an agreement was reached, and the Nantucket whaleman was released. But his health had been so seriously undermined by his imprisonment that he died before he could reach the coast and embark for home. Back in Nantucket, his widow, Lydia Gardner Bunker, and his seven children were to mourn his passing.

But the tragedy besetting this family did not end here. At the outbreak of the Anglo-French War, Captain Bunker's eldest son, Captain Obed Bunker, while in command of the Rotch ship *Greyhound,* was captured by a Dutch privateer in Delagoa Bay, on the east coast of Africa. Only a few years after Captain Peleg's death in France, his son Captain Tristram Bunker, while on a voyage to the Pacific Ocean as master of the London whaler *Scorpion,* went ashore in a small port on the coast of Chili and was attacked by desperadoes and killed.

In light of such family disasters, the story of the courageous widow Bunker, with her surviving family, makes an interesting contrast to the success (financially and socially) of her neighbors. The walk—as the railed platform on the roof was always called, and *not* the "widow's walk"—once found eager faces scanning the horizon with long-glasses, hoping to identify the familiar flag of the long awaited ship. But it is probable that the Widow Bunker never went up to the observation post after the news of her great loss.

There is a starkness to such episodes in Nantucket's history. But, notwithstanding the tragic overtones, the courage of these women, who continued to carry out their responsibilities as household heads, brings out some of the greatest pages in Nantucket's history.

The tall steeple of the Baptist Church on Summer Street is typical of many New England meeting houses, with a graceful white spire rising high above the rooftops. The church was built in 1840; the tower and steeple were added the following year. The bell, weighing 1,600 pounds and cast by Menely & Co. in Troy, was brought to the island from New York in 1854 aboard the schooner *Mary Jane* by Captain Fitzgerald. In the 1930's, when money was needed to repaint the graceful spire, the expense was underwritten by a neighbor, the Rev. Fr. Joseph M. Griffin, prelate of the Roman Catholic Church on Nantucket. Twenty years later, when the steeple needed vital structural repairs, a successful drive for funds was conducted by the Rev. William E. Gardner, a retired Episcopal minister. The Christian philosophy of brotherhood, so ably carried out by the Society of Friends on Nantucket, is characteristic of the island life.

Close by the Baptist Church is No. 7 Summer Street, a typical dwelling of the 1790 period, with center chimney, four-bayed front, and ells on the east end and rear. The doorway is a splendid example of the adaptation of a Greek Revival design for an eighteenth-century house. With its shingled sides, small-paned windows, and ridge chimney, it presents the simple lines of a typical home of its time.

Baptist Church Steeple. Summer Street.

Philip Macy House. 7 Summer Street.

Philip Macy's brother and partner, Isaac, lived only a stone's throw away, on Pleasant Street. The Macy brothers were closely associated all through their lives, in both business and private life. A century and a half ago an observer would have noticed two merchants who, morning and evening, walked together to and from their place of business on Straight Wharf. Isaac and Philip Macy displayed the same fraternal attachment that marked their father and uncle, Thomas and Peter Macy, and their grandfather and great-uncle, Obed and Silvanus Macy—an hereditary characteristic held by three successive sets of brothers in the same general business of fitting out whaleships and trading in coasting vessels. It was the example of these Quaker merchants which was so aptly followed and which gave rise to the island simile: "As close as the Macy brothers."

Though Philip was content with the traditional dwelling on Summer Street, Isaac, on the other hand, in keeping with many of his contemporaries, decided to build a Greek Revival house down the lane on Pleasant Street. (See p. 52.) There was no friction in their decisions, merely recognition that, despite their fraternal habits, their respective wives were entitled to follow their individual desires.

At the head of Summer Street, facing east, is No. 3 Pleasant Street, erected at its location at the turn of the 1800's but bearing evidence of an earlier construction, as it appears typical of the small houses moved in from the older settlement of Sherborn. This was the home of a remarkable family. Samuel Folger, a young blacksmith, married Nancy Hiller, and here they raised a family of nine children. The youngest son, James A. Folger, was to take his place in his father's ship chandlery, a business in which the senior Folger had a prosperous career. But Nantucket suffered the great disaster of a fire in 1846. It not only destroyed the waterfront and business section of the town, including the Folger store, but hastened the decline of the island's sole industry—whaling.

Two years later, with Nantucket in the doldrums, word of the discovery of gold in California stimulated the islanders. In

James A. Folger House. 3 Pleasant Street.

1849 a dozen ships left the island for California; other vessels from nearby ports sailed with hundreds of Nantucket men aboard. Some four hundred enterprising islanders went to the gold fields, among them James A. Folger, who was barely fifteen years old. He joined two older brothers in San Francisco and together they made the overland journey to the gold fields.

But James A. Folger soon realized there were other ways to make his fortune. Returning to San Francisco he found his experience as a carpenter brought his service into demand. One of his first jobs was helping to erect a Coffee and Spice Mill on Powell Street for William H. Bovey. The latter became interested in the fifteen-year-old carpenter, and when Bovey's business prospered he invited young Folger to work for him. In time the Nantucket youth became a partner. Several years later he acquired the business and Folger's Coffee became a household word in San Francisco. The firm's reputation spread steadily and continues to be known nationally.

It was characteristic of James A. Folger that more than mere enterprise went into the development of his company. In July, 1888, he went east to pay a visit to his ancestral home in Nantucket. It was at this time that he wrote his sales manager in San Francisco: "I am more than delighted that our sales keep up so grandly. Do not know how to account for it except on the theory that we have struggled so long and so hard to show our customers that we wanted to deal squarely, and that money-making was always secondary to a good reputation."

The philosophy of James A. Folger laid the groundwork for one of the most flourishing business enterprises in the west. It continues as a family-managed firm, enjoying a well-deserved success.

As a counterpart to the success story of James Athearn Folger, it is in keeping to note that his elder brother, Henry C. Folger, returned east after his California adventure and eventually settled in New York City. Henry's son, Henry Clay Folger, became as interested in mineral oil as his grandfather Samuel had been in whale oil, and early in our own century became President of the Standard Oil Company of New Jersey. It was Henry Clay

Folger who gave this country and the world the magnificent Shakespeare Library in Washington, D.C.

Next door to the Samuel Folger home is the interesting doorway of a high mansion—No. 1 Pleasant Street. Built in 1837, its portico and long French windows marked it as an early departure in style from its neighbors. When Henry Macy completed it for William H. Crosby, son of Matthew Crosby, and his bride, Elizabeth Pinkham, the second oldest daughter of Captain Seth Pinkham, the town looked upon it as an ideal dwelling for the prosperous young whaling merchant and his beautiful wife.

It was a fine marriage. Many a delightful "social" was held in this home, for the Crosbys were royal hosts. The first Chickering piano on Nantucket is said to have been in the east drawing room. French windows, double parlors, silver doorknobs, marble mantles, and hand-blocked wallpaper were innovations enough, but when the Crosbys introduced frozen mousse to the island, it was startling indeed! In 1838 a financial reversal came to William Crosby when a disastrous fire destroyed a number of warehouses where vast quantities of his oil were stored. His loss was estimated at twenty-four thousand dollars. The Great Fire of 1846, less than a decade later, almost completely ruined him.

Thus, what had promised to be the opening of a highly successful chapter in the mercantile career of an enterprising young man became a financial handicap, and the house passed from the young couple's possession within a few years of its erection. The prosperity of the whaling merchants often hinged on the whim of the elements; the unusual circumstances which ruined the young man were beyond any possible anticipation.

Across the street, on the southeast corner of Summer and Pleasant, is a small house situated well back from the sidewalk. It was originally a cooper shop and was converted into a comfortable home a half century ago; one of the old pumps remains located just under a front window. For a number of years it was the home of Colonel Lawrence Cummings, who had served as Chief of Staff for General Edwards of the Yankee Division in World War I. He joined the American Ambulance Corps in

William Crosby House. 1 Pleasant Street.

France in 1915, but with our entrance into the war, he enlisted in the Twenty-Sixth Division. He won his promotion under fire.

Because of his age he was not able to participate in World War II, so he accepted a post in Nantucket and organized the Civilian Aircraft Spotter's Group. On one occasion, while inspecting a spotter's station on the outskirts of town, he found the observer on midnight watch fast asleep.

"He was one of the town's prominent citizens," recounted Colonel Cummings, "and I felt it my duty to rudely awake him and lecture him on his responsibility as a sky-watcher. I had launched well into my impassioned harangue when I suddenly became aware that he had fallen asleep again! There wasn't any more to do but stay there until the end of his watch. At that precise moment he promptly awoke, bade me goodnight, and disappeared into the darkness. To cap the story, the replacement was nearly an hour late in reporting!"

Next door, the large house with the high basement is of the transitional style. It was built in 1820 by John Coleman, and for a number of years was the summer home of William O. Stevens, who wrote a number of books on historic places. One was *Nantucket—Far Away Island,* which he also illustrated with charming pen and ink sketches.

The adjoining house—No. 8 Pleasant Street—is an island treasure. It was built in 1785 for Walter Folger, Jr., and his bride, Anna Ray. Walter Folger was an island genius. Inventor, surveyor, lawyer, town official, and teacher, he possessed all the talents which characterized his Folger cousin, Benjamin Franklin; it was here he designed and completed his famous astronomical clock—a tall, or grandfather clock—which has continued to delight those who see it exhibited at the Peter Foulger Museum.

A man of great intellect, Walter Folger, Jr., was a mathematician and surveyor of note; an astronomer who built his own telescope; a lawyer and a legislator at the Congress in Washington; and a philosopher and historian. He was born in 1765 and died in 1849.

In 1850 the house was purchased by Captain Charles Starbuck; and it was here that Molly Starbuck, author of the island chronicle *My House and I,* was born. It was also the home of Captain James Wyer, who married the widow of Captain Starbuck. Both men were whaling masters and made voyages in the *Spartan* and *Islander.*

Mary E. (Molly) Starbuck's book, *My House and I,* is an island classic. Its pages reflect a Nantucket age which will never return: the time when the whaling era ended and a new business —"summer folks"—created a new way of life for the islanders. Miss Starbuck's poems and short stories were true word pictures of her time; the peace of her garden, the satisfaction gained from her circle of friends, and her pride in her home have given her book a permanent place in the history of Nantucket.

The little doorway beckons. As we approach to lift the knocker we may expect the door to slowly open and a sweet-toned voice welcome us in for a visit. Seated before a driftwood fire, with the flames tinged with the translucent colors of copper sheathing nails, Molly Starbuck's friends enjoyed winter afternoons when, after a stimulating conversation, they would partake in her collation of gingerbread and cream and oolong tea.

No. 7 Pleasant Street is one of the earliest wooden structures built in the Greek Revival style. With its handsome portico, center doorway with sidelights, parapet over cornice, and balustrade inlets, it attracts the eye. John Coleman built this house for Isaac Macy, brother of Philip, in 1825; a few years later Coleman constructed a similar house, No. 9, for Benjamin Easton. The latter was sold by the Easton heirs to the beloved Catholic priest Rev. Fr. Joseph M. Griffin in 1909, and it became the parsonage of St. Mary's Church for two decades.

Just before 1800 Obed Macy built his dwelling at 15 Pleasant Street; it is a structure with two chimneys above the ridge pole instead of the usual one. This is truly a house of history, as it was within that Obed Macy, the Quaker historian, wrote the first extensive history of Nantucket.

Molly Starbuck House. 8 Pleasant Street.

Isaac Macy House. 7 Pleasant Street.

Obed Macy House. 15 Pleasant Street.

There is a certain square solidarity to this house and this doorway. It is both an entranceway to history and an introduction to a way of life. Melville, in his classic *Moby-Dick,* alludes to Macy as "the worthy Obed," and quotes from his *History,* citing him as the "sole historian of Nantucket," which at that time was true.

Obed Macy was a birthright member of the Society of Friends, and his life was an example of the way in which the islanders applied their religious teachings to the everyday routines of their lives. Of a large family, Obed had few opportunities for an education, but he made the most of them. During the Revolution he labored as a farmhand, then learned the shoemaking trade. He made three short whaling voyages, but the life did not appeal to him, and he went into partnership with his brothers Silvanus and Barzillai Macy. Obed married Abigail Pinkham and Silvanus married her sister Anna. Obed and Silvanus were partners for forty-seven years and made modest fortunes in the boat-building and shipfitting business; they invested in whaleships and the coasting trade as well. During the French War of 1898 and the War of 1812, the brothers lost considerable money by seizures of whaleships, but nothing ever destroyed their fraternal bond— they were always partners. Obed's systematic and precise habits led to his keeping of a diary which, with his natural aptitude for retaining memories, formed the basis for his important *History.* Each of his four sons learned a trade as they grew to manhood—cooper, blacksmith, etc. The founder of Macy's, the great New York store, was Rowland H. Macy, grandson of Silvanus and great-nephew of Obed Macy.

Next door, at the corner of Mill Street, Obed's son Peter departed from the traditions of building (like others of his generation) and in 1846 constructed the Greek Revival dwelling at 17 Pleasant Street. The side entrance portico, with an Ionic column, pilasters at the corners, and clapboard siding, is similar to the General George Macy house on upper Main Street.

Peter Macy House. 17 Pleasant Street.

Obed Macy's 1790-style house, the 1750-dwelling to the north, and son Peter's to the south offer three distinct periods of island architecture.

The length of Pleasant Street from Main to Mill Streets "has always been a favorite section for residences," wrote Henry B. Worth, the historian, in 1906, "but the houses now standing are mostly built after the Revolution. Several have the large center chimney and were built about 1800."

The brick mansion on Pleasant Street, corner of Mill, has been known as "Moors' End" for three quarters of a century. The handsome estate, situated at the edge of the neat town, under the slope of the Mill Hills, has been fortunate in having families live within who appreciated it. It was built in 1827 by Jared Coffin, a young whale oil merchant, who had been successful in ventures in whaleships. He owned the majority of shares in the *Montano* and *Daniel Webster,* among others. He acquired the land between Mill Street and Candlehouse Lane (now erroneously called Angora Street) in 1820 and built the house in 1827. But Mrs. Coffin wished to live closer to the center of the town, so he sold his Pleasant Street mansion and erected an imposing three-story brick house on Broad Street. However, the same year this house was completed he sold it and moved to the vicinity of Boston.

Reuben Hallett made Moors' End his home for twenty years. In 1873, at the period of the island's lowest financial ebb, Jared Gardner purchased the brick mansion at auction for the sum of $2,350—an almost incredible figure but an indication of the local depression. One of the subsequent owners, H. B. Williams, laid out the garden more carefully and built the high brick wall. Another owner bought some handsome carriages and horses for the stable, while Edward F. Sanderson, who purchased the place in the early 1920's, carried out extensive renovations and gave the beautiful garden its formal look. Colonel Robert W. Stewart added a library in the Mill Street wing. The present owner, Mrs. Allan Melhado, has added her own touches to the beauty of the house.

"Moors' End." Pleasant Street.

The doorway is especially handsome, with its sidelights, semi-circular green fan with gilt eagle, brick stoop, brownstone steps, and iron railing. We may watch Mr. and Mrs. Coffin as they greet their guests, the scene being indicative of the second peak in Nantucket's whaling fortune. Other merchants, recognizing the social significance of this brick mansion, soon decided to build their own.

Cyrus Hussey House. 25 Pleasant Street.

There is a house of the lean-to style at the corner of Pleasant and South Mill Streets, facing south at a slight angle to the principle street, which has more than its expected share of adventures connected with the whale fishery. For here Cyrus Hussey was born. At sixteen he sailed as a cooper's assistant on board the whaleship *Globe*. During the voyage, while in the mid-Pacific, a young boatsteerer named Samuel Comstock organized a mutiny; in the space of an hour Captain Worth and two of his officers were murdered, the third mate succumbing the next morning. Comstock took the ship to the Mulgrave Islands, where he intended to establish a miniature island kingdom. The mutineers quarreled and Comstock was killed. Five of the faithful hands escaped with the ship, leaving the rest of the crew marooned with the mutineers. The natives, disgusted with the actions of the white men, attacked the camp one night and massacred all but two of the younger men—Cyrus Hussey and William Lay. After two years as captives, the two survivors were rescued by the U.S. Navy schooner *Dolphin,* under Captain "Mad Jack" Percival, which was dispatched from Valparaiso after the *Globe* had safely arrived there.

Cyrus Hussey returned to Nantucket in 1827, after four years absence. He remained home for only a period of a few months before shipping out again on another whaleship—and never came back. A century and a quarter later the great-granddaughter of Lieutenant Hiram Paulding, who had led the party rescuing Cyrus Hussey, came to Nantucket to visit and, in this house, met the great-grandniece of Hussey. The meeting had been arranged by a Nantucket man who had written a fictional account of the *Globe* and Hussey entitled *Mutiny at Midnight*.

Built in 1745, the house was owned by Stephen Chase, whose daughter Margaret inherited the house after marrying Crispus Gardner. Their daughter Lydia married Cyrus Hussey, the elder; their daughter Margaret married George Cary, whose descendants continued ownership through the Caldwells. The house had been in the family line for over two hundred years, and the restoration of it in recent times by its new owners has guaranteed its permanency for many years to come.

Milk Street has a range of house types which are typical of two centuries, and every one has its particular story to tell. On the corner of Quaker Road—33 Milk Street—is a typical Nantucket house, a two and a half-story dwelling built by George Coffin in 1820. One of his daughters married Captain William B. Gardner, master of both the whaleship *Columbus* and the merchantman *Sarah Parker.* One of his sons, Arthur H. Gardner, was born while Mrs. Gardner was aboard the latter ship on a voyage to the west coast of the United States. He returned to spend his life at 33 Milk Street, becoming the editor of *The Nantucket Journal,* a successful newspaper, as well as a representative to the State Legislature from Nantucket and the Treasurer of the town. Upon Arthur Gardner's death, his wife took over the duties of that office, becoming the first island woman to serve in that capacity. Grace Brown Gardner, their daughter, after a busy career as a teacher on the mainland, retired to her ancestral home, and here she compiled a series of remarkable scrapbooks, now preserved at the Historical Association's library. The house remained in the Gardner family until 1974—successively owned by a family clan for over a hundred and fifty years.

Across the street, at No. 26 Milk Street, is the little house lived in by Captain Isaiah Folger. The owner and skipper of a trading schooner named the *Exact,* Captain Folger was caught by the California Gold Rush fever in 1850 and decided to take his little schooner around Cape Horn to San Francisco. Upon arrival in California, however, he decided to become a coastal trader and made voyages along the coast. One day in November, 1851, while lying in the harbor of Portland, Oregon, he was approached by a group of pioneer settlers who wished to be taken up Puget Sound, there to rendezvous with a companion group. A few days later, Captain Folger rowed his passengers ashore to a place called Alki Point, where they met the second group. These were the founders of the present city of Seattle, Washington; the little Nantucket schooner *Exact* had become a nineteenth-century *Mayflower.*

Isaiah Folger House. 26 Milk Street.

Before returning home Captain Folger sold his little schooner, and several years later she was wrecked during a storm that drove her ashore just above the Golden Gate. In his retiring years, the captain opened a small grocery store at the corner of New Mill and Milk Streets. As we observe the pleasant appearing front door of this old dwelling we may feel the satisfaction of Captain Isaiah, returning from the dangers of his trade to pursue the humble vocation of shopkeeper, content to be home with his family and friends after adventures in other parts of America.

The typical two-story dwelling at 11 Milk Street is a house of two ages, the older section having been moved into new Sherborn from old Sherborn as early as 1780. The doorway front entrance is at a slight angle to the street, following the custom of the time, when the owners sought to take advantage of all the space available in the house lot. The side garden near the second doorway is especially charming.

Here Joseph Starbuck was born. By considerable drive and business acumen he became one of the most prominent of the early nineteenth-century whale oil merchants. He built a substantial mansion on New Dollar Lane, and in 1837 financed the construction of three brick dwellings on Main Street for his three sons—George, Matthew, and William—which have become known as the "Three Bricks." Among the ships in which Joseph Starbuck owned the majority of shares were the *President,* *Omega, Young Hero,* and *Three Brothers,* all of which were highly successful under responsible shipmasters. One of his great disappointments was the loss of a new ship named for himself. After one outstanding voyage, the *Joseph Starbuck* was lost in a gale at the entrance to Nantucket Harbor, caught by the storm as she was starting across Nantucket Sound for a completion of her outfitting at Edgartown.

As we study the front doorways of these island dwellings, and examine their details, we note that while certain features may mark all, there is still a difference. This is as it should be, as belonging to the Nantucket family of houses they may bear a resemblance without being exactly alike. Coupled with such an

Joseph Starbuck House. 11 Milk Street.

architectural background there is also the fact of the changes made by successive owners over the years.

At the corner of Main Street and Gardner in Monument Square are two houses of ancient vintage. That numbered 105 Main Street is actually of two ages, the eastern section being of 1690. It was moved in from old Sherborn when Christopher Starbuck built the enlarged dwelling in 1720, at the time Queen Street (now Gardner Street) was laid out. There is a distinct aura of age about the front entrance, an excellent preparation for the interior, with its huge fireplaces, wide floorboards, exposed corner posts, and summer beams.

The intangible quality of the olden time clings to this house. It reminds one of the actual reason for the creation of the old town. When the children of the first settlers recognized that their livelihood was in the sea rather than on the land, they began to build the new Sherborn around the Great Harbor, which was a necessity for ships and shipping. With the establishment of the new colonial industry—the Southern Whale Fishery—the town grew steadily, marking each decade with new streets and new houses. The period between 1720 to 1775 was one in which the burgeoning business of whaling was reflected by the growth of the town.

Some changes in old houses have literally disguised their oldness, and when the central chimney at 107 Main Street was altered, and the lean-to roof line changed by the additions to the north, the dwelling lost its original look of age. Zaccheus Macy built it here in 1748, and his boat-builder's shop was probably off the little court in the rear. Zaccheus became known as the "bone-setter." Despite his lack of medical training he developed superior skill as a physician in caring for broken bones. As a Quaker he carried on this unusual avocation without charge. It is estimated that, during his life, he replaced dislocations and set broken bones to the number of some two thousand cases—yet he never accepted money or any remuneration. Upon retiring from business life he took up farming; being civic-minded, he also served as Town Treasurer, Assessor, and Selectman and held the post of Wharfinger at Straight and South Wharves for many years.

Christopher Starbuck House. 105 Main Street.

Reuben Joy House. 107 Main Street.

Captain Reuben Joy, who succeeded Macy in ownership of the house, was one of the sealers who made mysterious voyages to the Falklands, to Patagonia, and to other little-known regions. His son, Captain Obed Joy, was born here in 1763 and went into the Pacific Ocean with the first American whalemen from the island. He took command of the Ship *Atlas* in 1803, and on one voyage successfully escaped from a British frigate then impressing Yankee seamen. When Stephen West and Cliff Cronwinshield, of Salem, fitted out the ship *Minerva* for sailing early in the nineteenth century, they secured Captain Mayhew Folger of Nantucket as her master. Captain Folger declared he would make the voyage if Captain Joy sailed with him, because the latter knew more about sealing than he. Captain Joy was engaged. The *Minerva* not only made a successful voyage but was the first Salem craft to circumnavigate the world. Captain Mayhew Folger afterward took command of the *Topaz*, of Boston, and on this voyage (1808) stopped at Pitcairn Island, where he was the first to discover what had happened to the H.M.S. *Bounty* and the runaway mutineers.

The front entrance of the Macy-Joy house is of a century ago (1878), so it bears little resemblance to the original. However, it is included in this study to show how change may bring a graceful transition.

Main Street would be expected to have its proportionate share of shipmasters and sailormen. From Bloom Street to the Monument there are some houses whose stories are a part of the island's maritime history. The doorway at 117 Main Street once witnessed the unusual sight of two Chinese visitors being ushered in as the guests of Captain Cary, the owner of the house. The Orientals were Wing Cher, a merchant of Canton (the only Chinese port open to foreigners in that huge country), and his servant. Both were dressed in their flowing garments of rich hues, in marked contrast to the sober brown clothing of their Quaker hosts. The year was 1808, and Captain Jonathan Paddack had just returned from a voyage to China in the ship *Favourite*, having sold a cargo of seal skins at Canton and returning with Chinese goods and eighty thousand dollars in gold. The owners of the ship had not only being delighted with Captain Paddack's success but were highly pleased that Wing Cher had agreed to come to Nantucket to discuss further trade.

The Nantucket adventurers underwriting such voyages (and usually the master of the ship was one) hoped to obtain more financial support from their fellow islanders for other such voyages. However, Nantucket was wedded to whaling and the losing experience of another voyage to China (in the ship *Rose*) had the effect of discouraging potential investors and similar efforts were abandoned. Thus, the island lost a golden opportunity to enter in that trade with China which was to bring such wealth to Boston, New York, and Philadelphia.

As an honored guest of the Cary family, Wing Cher had the opportunity not only to learn of this whaling capital of America but to see firsthand the Quaker influence in the island community. Did he not find that the Society of Friends with their philosophy of Christianity had much in common with the Buddhist religion of China? Only those who entered and left this portal would ever have the occasion to record such, and unfortunately they left no account. The graceful entrance and stoop must have made a perfect stage and setting for such a tableau, but we must supply our own detail, allowing it to be as dramatic and colorful as the bare facts themselves convey.

Quite another facet in island history is brought out through the history of the house across the way—120 Main Street. Captain Thomas Paddack, after a successful voyage around Cape Horn, began this square structure in 1807. The war of 1812 began while the fleet was in the South Seas, and they were trapped as they attempted to return through the powerful blockade of the Royal Navy along the coast. Captain Paddack sailed his ship, the *Perseveranda,* all the way from South America's west coast to within sight of home, but was captured near Tuckernuck Shoal by a British frigate in November, 1814, only miles from the safety of the home harbor.

As he climbed the steps leading to this front door the weight of the disaster must have added years to his bent shoulders. So close to safety, so close to another great success and a near impossible accomplishment, and all ending with the flash of a frigate's guns, forcing him to heave to with Nantucket under his lee. We look at this entrance with a sigh. The whims of fate are especially poignant when we reflect upon the "mariner home from the sea" under such circumstances.

As we stop before the front steps of 109 Main Street we note the architectural differences between this house, built in 1830 for Captain Reuben Joy II, and its neighbors. A century age we would have gone up the stoop and entered the doorway to be

Edward Cary House. 117 Main Street.

greeted by a sprightly lady, whose gray locks would bob as she described the contents of the unique museum she kept in her front rooms. Eliza Ann McCleave, wife of Captain Robert Mc-Cleave, not only survived her husband by two decades but made her livelihood by displaying many of the shells, baskets, shawls, fans, scrimshaw, and other mementos he had brought home with him from voyages to the South Seas and the Orient.

At one time she had watched her husband walk down these steps on the eve of a voyage he never expected to make. It was in the early winter of 1838, and Robert McCleave had again been given command of the ship *Rambler;* he had served first as mate and then as master on two successive voyages. But this was to be a voyage that would launch a chapter in American maritime history, for Captain McCleave had as a special passenger one of the ship's owners, Frederick Coleman Sanford, who was acting as an emissary of the United States Department of State.

For several years Sanford had petitioned the government to install a U.S. Consulate in New Zealand. Since the beginning of the century this remote part of the world had been frequented by American whaleships, led by the pioneer Nantucketers, and the need of a representative of this country in that land was becoming evident. Upon the recommendation of Sanford and a few others who knew the situation, Secretary Forsyth, with congressional approval, appointed James B. Clendon, an English resident of New Zealand, as the first U.S. Consul there. The *Rambler* carried the official papers, seal, library, and other necessary materials, which Sanford brought ashore at Russell, in the Bay of Islands, North Island. There, in May, 1839, the home of Mr. Clendon became the first United States Consulate. Among those present at the initial ceremony were Captain McCleave, Frederick Sanford, and Captain Sir Francis Baxter, of the French ship *Orion,* which was then in the harbor. Three Nantucketers thus were on hand for the occasion.

Returning from that voyage after an absence of three years and eleven months, Captain McCleave brought with him yet another group of curios for his wife's collections. In later years, after his passing, when her museum became her means of liveli-

Robert McCleave House. 109 Main Street.

hood, summer visitors made repeated trips to this house, climbed the steps and listened to Eliza tell stories of the relics displayed. Her knowledge of the faraway places which each piece represented was remarkable. The collection reflected both the enterprise of her mariner husband and the many parts of the watery world with direct Nantucket connections.

The architectural period known as the Greek Revival came to Nantucket at the time it was enjoying the second great peak in its whaling prosperity (1830-1845); many of the wealthy ship owners built their imposing mansions at this time. Many of the older houses reflected the new style during this opulent period merely by having their old doorways changed. Among these is that of 102 Main Street.

Captain James Bunker was a whaleman who enjoyed the fruits of his good deeds. Many a shipmaster out of Nantucket had performed acts of kindness by rescuing castaways or ships in distress in the open sea, but Captain Bunker received an unexpected dividend from an act of charity. In the year 1816, while in command of the whaleship *Tarquin*, he sighted a ship in the South Atlantic flying signals of distress. Heaving to, Captain Bunker sent out one of his whaleboats; the master of the disabled craft returned to the *Tarquin*, bringing the account of his troubles. The vessel was the Portuguese frigate *Sacramento*. Two weeks before she had been caught in a hurricane and suffered extensive damage; she was now helpless. On board was a company of soldiers under the command of a General Selvaro; the frigate had been bound for Montevideo, which was then at war with Brazil. Captain Bunker offered to take the company off and sail for Santos, the nearest port, but General Selvaro offered to reward the whaler if he would escort the frigate.

The bargain was made. Captain Bunker requested that the Portuguese government fill his ship with oil; he also asked that he be allowed freedom to take whales close in to the coast of Brazil. Upon reaching Rio de Janeiro, however (after being driven off shore from Santos by a gale), the *Tarquin* was given only nine hundred barrels of oil, and it had taken months of

James Bunker House. 102 Main Street.

negotiations with the Court of King John (the Portuguese king who had been driven from Portugal and had set up his government in Brazil). As General Selvaro had been dispatched to the scene of the war, he was not able to help press the claim, so Captain Bunker finally found an ally in Major Cottrell, an Irish soldier-of-fortune who had married a Portuguese lady and was on the disabled frigate at the time of the *Tarquin*'s timely aid. Through his wife's efforts Major Cottrell gained an audience with King John and the king agreed to carry out General Selvaro's bargain. Although nine hundred barrels was then placed aboard the *Tarquin*, it was not enough to fill the ship, and Captain Bunker issued a formal claim through the American Consul at Rio.

Thirty-five years later the Portuguese government in Lisbon awarded the *Tarquin* the sum of sixty-eight thousand dollars for helping save the *Sacramento*, and the money was divided among the officers and crew. But by this time there were only four of the Nantucketers still living, and Captain Bunker was not among them. Nonetheless, the survivors voted to present his share to his family.

In the year 1863, Captain Joseph Mitchell returned to his Nantucket home after an absence of a decade. Like most Nantucket men he had gone to sea as a young whaleman and worked his way aft to become master of his ship. Going to sea at fourteen, Mitchell became captain at twenty-eight, and after a quarter of a century as a whaling master he went to California in the Gold Rush of 1850-51. But in San Francisco he found opportunity in taking command of ships rather than in the gold fields. And for several years he commanded ships bound to and from San Francisco, one being the *Telassar*.

Now he was back, to retire with a competency at the age of fifty-two, and he sought a suitable home. He purchased 100 Main Street, the clapboard and shingle house which William Hadwen had remodeled in 1840. (Only a few years before he had had Brown Coleman build the Greek Revival mansion on the corner of Main and Pleasant Streets; it is now known as the Hadwen-

Satler House.) Captain Mitchell liked his new house. It was actually of two ages: the front or main house was constructed by the Barney family in 1800, at which time the old house had been moved to the rear as an addition.

The front door, with its pilaster Green Revival design and sidelights, was especially pleasing to him. It was noted by Captain Mitchell's contemporaries that he often paused to stand a moment in the doorway before entering or leaving. With his ivory-headed cane, beaver hat, and flowered waistcoat, he personified the successful shipmaster who had won his comfortable retirement by hard work.

Whenever he was with a close circle of friends he could be prevailed upon to tell of one of his experiences when in command of the Starbuck whaleship *Three Brothers.* It was in August, 1847, when the ship hove to off the romantic island of Pitcairn. "My ship lay off and on for a week," he said, "and the islanders helped my crew take off two hundred barrels of water, one hundred and fifty pounds of yams, and as many barrels of potatoes, together with a quantity of fruit. I paid them well and I have since been told by Captain Palmer and others that visited the island that they remembered my kindness and often offered prayers for my safety. The head man told me the whole story of the *Bounty* mutiny as it had been handed down through generations. A sixteen-year-old girl named Martha Young wrote out in detail how the young ladies of Pitcairn spent their day. Rising at six each morning, they spent the first half hour in prayer and reading. It took one minute to comb their hair, fifteen minutes to feed the hogs, and an equal amount of time to make a garland for their dress. The next three hours were spent in gathering provisions from the mountain fields, followed by two hours of work in the fields. Schoolwork took the next five hours, followed by one hour devoted to washing and mending clothes. Fishing for squid took at least fifteen minutes, and the time allotted for courting was two and one-half hours. For sleep, seven hours were allowed; the two hours and fourteen minutes left in the twenty-four were given up to music or singing."

On this voyage in the *Three Brothers,* Captain Mitchell was

Joseph Mitchell House. 100 Main Street.

gone for five years and eight days. In his *Journal* of this ship, which is fortunately preserved at the Peter Foulger Museum, Nantucket Historical Association, he wrote at the conclusion of one day's entry:

I am in hopes to see whales soon and get some. We are now fifty-one months from home—is it possible that I have been that long separated from my wife? . . . I dreamed last night that I was home, among civilized beings, taking all the comfort imaginable, and thinking how thankful I was to get clear of this whaleship and all that was in her. But in the midst of my dream I awoke and, behold, here I was still aboard the old blubber hunter. . . . I have spent fifteen years on board of her, the best years of my life. . . .

It was at the conclusion of this long voyage that Captain Mitchell embarked for California; his fortunes changed, and within the next decade he accumulated enough money to retire, return home, and purchase this handsome mansion, where he spent many happy years among his family and friends.

The charm of Main Street is in the inherent qualities of its historic old dwellings and classic mansions, which reflect a harmony of style and quiet appeal. When we find a combination of designs that blend to become an architectural jewel, the result is pleasing to both the trained observer and the appreciative layman. Such a house is No. 99 Main Street.

This, too, is a house of two eras. The older section was originally built by Valentine Swain in 1771; the renovated dwelling was constructed in 1830 for Thomas Macy. The doorway, with its handsome proportions, sidelights, and graceful fan with carved eagle, makes the Federal-style clapboard structure one of the most photographed in the town.

Thomas Macy was a son of Obed Macy, the historian. He learned both the cooper's and blacksmith's trade at his father's direction and then invested in various enterprises. He gradually extended his business interests and by 1824, at the time of his second marriage (to Eunice Coffin), he owned the majority of shares in a number of whaleships. Two of his best investments were made in the voyages of the well-known whaleships *Potomac* and *Mohawk*. He was a man of considerable personal appeal and was much sought after to serve as moderator at town meetings and other public gatherings. He was a Quaker, a strong Whig, and served as Postmaster under President Monroe. His sons, Isaac and Philip, carried on the family tradition of fraternal affection.

During his tenure as Postmaster he became incensed at the number of letters being placed on whaleships bound for the South Seas by "off-islanders" who were taking advantage of the "free" service. He placed a notice in the Nantucket newspaper, reading:

Having received sundry letters for missionaries at the Sandwich Islands enclosed to the Postmaster, to be by him forwarded by whaleships from

Thomas Macy House. 99 Main Street.

this port, without even the formality of "Please forward," I think it proper to state that persons wishing to send letters to the Sandwich Islands must pay postage . . . and those wishing to use the illegal sanction of my name to evade the payment of legal postage may rest assured that their letters are much more likely to be perused at the General Post Office in Washington than at the Sandwich Islands, even if they come all the way from Kentucky.

Thomas Macy, Postmaster
Nantucket, Sept. 3, 1822

In the mid-1800's that section of Main Street between Pleasant and Pine came to be known as the "Court End," as most of the houses were newly constructed and were of the classical or Georgian style, though a few Federalist Period dwellings and some renovated older houses were there for good measure. The Starbucks, Coffins, Hadwens, Barneys, Swifts, Crosbys, and Swains had such a close family relationship that it was truly a neighborhood of "in-laws"—with the added connections of business partnerships as well. Social affairs were thus also family gatherings; during the 1840's one of these groups, meeting regularly, called itself "The Budget," and kept a record of some of its activities.

William Hadwen engaged Frederick Brown Coleman to build the two white-pillared Greek Revival mansions here in 1844 and 1845, retaining the corner house as his home and presenting its handsome companion to his niece, Mary G. Swain, who married a young man from the mainland named George W. Wright. A few years after the couple took up residence, the California Gold Rush aroused their interest and they went to San Francisco. Wright became interested in politics and became the first congressman elected to the National Congress by the new State of California. Among other owners of the residence was Allen Coffin, an island attorney, who made a number of contributions to Nantucket historical writings.

A number of visitors to the island, during a walk up Main Street in the summer of 1822, saw a group of people gathered on the wide porch of the Hadwen House, framed by the graceful

The Hadwen Houses, 98 and 96 Main Street.

Lower floor rooms of the Hadwen-Satler House.

portico. "What is the occasion?" asked one of the visitors, addressing a lady standing nearby, who was also watching the scene. "Oh, it's a wedding," was her polite but terse reply. "Who are the bride and groom?" came the next natural query. " 'Tis William Hadwen's adopted daughter, Anna Ray," was the prompt response; "she's marrying an off-islander." It was not until some time later that the visitors learned that the off-islander happened to be Oliver Ames, the Governor of Massachusetts!

Frederick Brown Coleman, son of Barnabas, had a rare gift as an architect. He was an excellent craftsman as well, and so scrupulous in his honesty that he cheated no one but himself. In his old age, he and his wife were compelled to seek refuge at their son's farm in Ohio. When the owners of the homes he had built learned of "Uncle Brown's penniless circumstances," they contributed $1,760 toward a fund to ease the last days of this conscientious island builder. John Coleman, his brother, was a skilled carpenter, too, but was a more shrewd businessman. The Hadwen-Satler House is now owned by the Historical Society and open to the public.

When Joseph Starbuck, the most successful whaling merchant of his time, took his three sons into partnership in 1833 he launched a new ship, quite fittingly named the *Three Brothers*. She made seven consecutive voyages from 1833 to 1865. Before the return of the ship from her maiden voyage Joseph Starbuck had purchased two estates and a store on Main Street; he had cleared the land and erected thereon three brick mansions. Of the Federal-Greek Revival style, with four end chimneys, square cupolas, recessed center front doorways, Ionic porticos, granite steps, and iron fences, they were identical in interior as well as exterior design. They were soon named the "Three Bricks," and are still known as such.

The middle "Brick" became the home of the middle son— Matthew Starbuck—who became the true successor of his father in the business. The house is the only one still in the possession of descendants of the Starbuck family. James Childs, a master carpenter, and Christopher Capen, master mason, were engaged

Matthew Starbuck House. 95 Main Street.

for the construction work. The first house was completed in the autumn of 1837, and the two companion structures followed rapidly. Bricks for the walls and slate for the roof were brought to the island by Captain Henry Pinkham in the sloop *Enterprise;* other sloops transported the lumber. The entire cost for these three handsome houses was $40,124; this included the "freighting" as well as the building. While the three sons maintained their individual domiciles, Joseph did not convey the properties to them until the fall of 1850. Perhaps this was characteristic of Starbuck, for as a businessman he wished to control his own whaling firm, although the three sons were equal partners.

Matthew Starbuck's first wife died in 1838, three years after their marriage, but it was not until 1840 that he married again, bringing Catherine Wyer, the daughter of Captain Christopher Wyer, to the middle "Brick" as his bride. Five children were born at 95 Main Street between 1842 and 1850, and all came to know their grandfather Joseph, who died in March, 1861.

Not only did Matthew inherit the business sagacity of his father, but he carried on the firm until his retirement a few years before his death in 1876. His wife Catherine was keenly interested in the cultural life of the town, and when the famous Negro orator and writer Frederick Douglass came to Nantucket in 1886 for a lecture at the Unitarian Church, she opened her home for a reception to honor this remarkable man.

The pleasant residence at 91 Main Street is an excellent example of how an older dwelling may be converted into a spacious home, the work being done in 1820 for Henry Swift, who married Mary Coffin, daughter of Zenas. Three of the Coffin sisters lived within a few doors of each other in this section of Main Street. The doorway of this house is of the Greek Revival style, handsomely designed, with pilasters and sidelights, and set off by the well-proportioned fence.

One of the finest of the island's many gardens was created in the rear of this house by Harriet Pinkham Calder, wife of Timothy Calder. By the side yard, where a trellis was covered with red "Quarterly Meeting" roses and scented with honey-

Swift-Calder House. 91 Main Street.

suckle, the path led to the splendid garden in the rear. Here oblong beds of old-fashioned posies were edged by English box and separated by shell pathways; pinks, wallflowers, petunias, and mignonettes vied for attention; tall hollyhocks guarded fragrant beds of pennyroyal and the peppermint, thyme, sweet marjoram, sage, and savory grown for kitchen use. In the rear, by the Coffin School fence, fruit trees flourished with crocuses and hyacinths, sprays of Solomon seal and old-fashioned chrysanthemums.

In the Victorian Age the houses on Main Street in Nantucket had some of the most beautiful plantings imaginable. Ships returning from distant parts often brought slips of trees and flower bulbs for island gardens. The houses themselves reflected the "fragrance" of other worlds both outside and in. Linen closets with scent of lavender; Chinese jars of rose leaves; camphor-wood chests; and china closets, where spicy odors served as a delicate aromatic background for English and Chinese porcelain.

There was time then for leisure in the afternoon. The house-wife, with her regular chores completed, would have a few neighbors or friends in for tea; or perhaps she would put on her second-best dress and, with her sewing basket at hand, sit "under the window" in the front room and enjoy the time-honored Nantucket pastime of looking out into the pleasant vistas of Main Street and "watching the pass."

In viewing this old doorway it is pleasant, indeed, to visualize the ladies of the last century in their crinolines and bonnets walking sedately up Main Street to enter Elizabeth Calder's comfortable home for an afternoon tea hour. No doubt on a warm summer day they would pay a visit to the colorful garden as well, and wander through the flower-bordered paths, enjoying to the fullest the aroma of a hundred blooms in this fine old Nantucket garden.

At first glance the sturdy house numbered 89 Main Street appears similar to those dwellings built in the 1820's which are scattered throughout the town. However, the eastern section was of the lean-to style and was built originally in 1740. In the 1790's it was the home of Silvanus Macy, brother and business partner of Obed Macy, who has been mentioned.

In 1796 the town was stunned by the news that the first bank ever to be launched on the island—the Nantucket Bank—had been robbed of twenty thousand dollars worth of specie. The incident caused greater damage than the mere loss of money. Several prominent citizens, who were directors of the bank, were amazed when they became suspects; the town was wracked with tales of the accused and the accusers. Among those who exerted power was Silvanus Macy; he often held secret meetings, leading a group who privately investigated the robbery. Over a period of months, at night, this unofficial investigating group would individually make their way from their respective homes to Main Street and this house. We can see them now, dimly outlined in the darkness, as they approach the doorway, their faces only briefly shown as the heavy door opens and they enter for the secret conference. The Quaker control of island affairs went

Silvanus Macy House. 89 Main Street.

through a grave crisis at this time, and Silvanus Macy did not shirk his responsibility.

From his humble start as a mariner, Captain Silvanus Macy went on to become a partner with his brother Obed in a successful enterprise. A man of robust constitution, he was described by Obed as one who was never combative, but always respected. He lived in this house nearly forty years, regularly attending to his daily business along the waterfront. Since he had been a whaleman in his younger years and then commander of sloops in the coastal trade, bringing oil and candles to market, he, like his brother, brought sound knowledge to the firm. As agents for many whaleships, together they saw the island develop to its second whaling peak of prosperity in the early decades of the nineteenth century.

Standing at a slight angle to the roadway is 81 Main Street. It was built before the Revolution, but with its huge center chimney, two and one-half story clapboard front, and shingled sides, it is as sturdy a house as will be found in the town. Under its transom, the door is little changed from the original design, and the front steps, of wood, are of simple construction. The whole house has an air of dignity and repose.

On an early evening in June, 1821, Captain Christopher Burdick left his vessel—the schooner *Huntress*—at Old South Wharf to walk up Main Street to his home at No. 81. He had been gone for over a year, and his voyage had taken him to one of the most remote places in the world—the South Shetland Islands, four hundred miles south of Cape Horn and in the unknown regions of the Antarctic. The *Huntress* had been bound on a hunt for seals, the fur pelts of which were bringing high prices in Canton, China. In the Falkland Islands, a rendezvous for sealers as well as for whalers, Captain Burdick had met Captain John Davis, in the ship *Huron,* of New Haven, and the two shipmasters had agreed to sail to the South Shetlands in company, as there were then no charts of this obscurely known area.

As Captain Burdick entered his home that June evening he carried with him the logbook of his voyage on the *Huntress.* A

Christopher Burdick House. 81 Main Street.

century and a quarter later that logbook, straying from its Main Street home, was found in the attic of a little house in another part of the town. The recovery of this log made maritime history, for on its pages, under the date of February 1, 1821, was an entry describing a special cruise undertaken by Captain Burdick in search of new sealing grounds. It was on this day he sighted land to the south-southeast which he recorded as the coast of what he "supposed to be a continent." This was the first recognition of what came to be discovered as the last of the great continents—Antarctica. Later, the logbook of Captain Davis, his partner, revealed that he, too, a week earlier, had sighted this land. Thus, Antarctica was actually discovered (and recognized) by the humble sealers twenty years before the great explorers came upon its icy shores.

Captain Burdick was an outstanding navigator, and later owned a brig named after him, the *Christopher Burdick*. In 1831, while on a voyage to Central America for logwood, he was stricken with tropical fever and died. His faithful crew, true to his wishes, brought his body home preserved in a cask, and he was buried in the Prospect Hill Cemetery.

As Main Street curves away from the junction with Ray's Court it marks a small passageway on the left side leading to Liberty Street which is known as Walnut Lane. On the corner a high wooden residence, painted white, catches the eye. The recessed doorway is reached by a flight of stone steps; sidelights frame the heavy door. The older section of the house, the original occupant of the site, is now in the rear of the Greek Revival mansion that is 77 Main Street. It was erected in 1836 by John Shaw, a whaling merchant, who was a partner in a firm owning a candle factory nearby on Liberty Street.

During the 1880's and early 1890's the house was lived in by Charles Henry Webb, a journalist working in New York City whose pen name was "John Paul." Early in his career Webb became acquainted with Samuel Clemens, who was later to be known as Mark Twain. It was Webb who arranged for the publication of Twain's first successful short story, the now-famous

John Shaw House. 77 Main Street.

Charles G. Coffin House. 78 Main Street.

"Jumping Frog of Calaveras County." Later, the two writers had a serious falling out; but for this, it is possible that Mark Twain would have been among the number of distinguished authors visiting Webb's home.

In this century the house was the summer residence of Dr. Joseph Sidney Mitchell, a prominent Chicago physician; he was the first president of the Nantucket Historical Association. Mrs. Mitchell resided here after her husband's death, when it passed into the hands of her son, Leeds Mitchell; the house is still owned by that family.

The two brick mansions opposite each other at 75 and 78 Main Street were built in the early 1830's by Henry and Charles G. Coffin, who carried on the firm started by their father, Zenas Coffin. The Charles Coffin residence (No. 78) was built in 1831; Henry Coffin had the same workmen construct his home (No. 75) in 1833. Both were public-spirited men; Charles was one of the founders of the Atheneum Library, while Henry did much to encourage the planting of elm trees throughout the town.

The firm of Charles G. and Henry Coffin was among the last of the Nantucket whaling companies to close its books; its last ship—the *Constitution*—sailed in 1857 and was sold to New York upon its return home in 1863. Many of their vessels made notable voyages, the *Catawba,* the *Omega,* the *Peruvian,* and the *Zenas Coffin* among them. But one of their ships has a claim to literary as well as whaling fame; this was the one named for the two brothers—the *Charles & Henry.*

In the late fall of the year 1842, the ship was lying at Tahiti, and Captain John B. Coleman, disheartened by the poor quality of his boatsteerers (harpooners), signed on a young American he found ashore looking for a berth. In signing on the young man he wrote, in a bold hand, the name "Herman Melville." Melville was to serve until July of the next year (1843), when he received his honorable discharge at Lahaina, the port on the island of Maui in the Hawaiian Islands. From his experience on the *Charles & Henry* the author incorporated a number of passages in his books. It is to be noted that Captain Coleman received better treatment than the master of the *Acushnet,* Melville's first whaler.

Melville visited Nantucket in 1851, and during his walk up Main Street he passed between the two brick mansions of the men who gave their names to the last whaleship on which he sailed. Perhaps he was aware of this, although there is no record of his stopping by. He did, however, visit Thomas Macy at 99 Main Street, where he received a copy of Mr. Macy's father's *History of Nantucket,* a volume which he utilized in his writing of *Moby-Dick.* Melville's copy is now preserved at Princeton University.

In their close association over the years, Charles G. and Henry Coffin were the epitome of honorable businessmen, maintaining the tradition of a firm founded by their grandfather, Captain Micajah Coffin, and developed by Zenas Coffin, their father. Somehow, the durable qualities of the two brick mansions they built represent the stalwart character of their lives, and the fact that the respective doorways are quite different in design indicates they were individuals as well as brothers closely allied in family and business life.

Over the century and a half since its erection in 1820, the residence at 72 Main Street has changed little if any in its appearance, despite the fact that the life of the town has changed so drastically. One of the handsomest doorways in New England marks its facade. It has a high granite stoop and iron-railed steps on both sides leading up to the graceful portico and front door; the door itself is flanked by two Greek Ionic columns and framed by sidelights with transom.

John Wendell Barrett moved into the house with his bride, Lydia Mitchell Barrett, soon after the house was completed. She was the daughter of Christopher Mitchell, one of the old whaling merchants, whose firm spanned the years from the eighteenth into the nineteenth century. Barrett was a member of the firm of Barrett & Upton, whaling merchants and suppliers. He later became president of the Pacific Bank, which sits diagonally opposite his home.

When the Great Fire of 1846 was raging up through the business section of Main Street on that fateful July night, it appeared that nothing could prevent it from engulfing the Barrett mansion. Despite the pleas of his family and friends, Lydia Mitchell Barret refused to leave her home, saying in her Quaker manner that if the house was to be burned she wished to go with it. While the flames leaped high in the night sky, and the cries of the fire-fighters rang out, and the boom of bursting powder kegs, which were used to blow up buildings in the path of the fire, added terror to the scene, Mrs. Barrett sat in her front room —a silent watcher.

John W. Barrett House. 72 Main Street.

Then suddenly, as though by miraculous intervention, the wind shifted and the flames veered to the north, along Centre Street, and the Barrett mansion was saved. But Lydia Barrett did not collapse in reaction to this good fortune; instead she busied herself organizing supplies of food and coffee for the fire-fighters. Among those she served were officers and men from the U.S. vessels *Galatin* and *Wave,* which were then in the harbor; they had been dispatched ashore to lend invaluable aid to the Nantucket firemen and volunteers.

The successive owners of this fine old house have maintained it with true regard for its representation as a period piece in the historical study of the island. In fact, the preservation of many of the town's old houses by owners who have made Nantucket their second home has been one of the most important influences in shaping the present character of the town.

Masonic Hall. Main Street.

Just above the Pacific Bank on Main Street is a structure only recently restored which now serves as the Trust Department for the bank. For many years it was referred to as the Lodge Building, since it was built for the Masonic order in 1802; but long after it ceased to be its headquarters the name stayed with the building. Of Federalist Period style, with arched windows on the second floor and Roman Ionic pilasters flanking the center bay and outer corners, its first floor was remodeled into a Greek Revival Period store front in 1830. A number of shops occupied this portion of the building, including a grocery, stationery and notions shop, Western Union office, gift shop, and bookstore.

The Union Lodge of Masons is one of the earliest in the country, having been organized in 1771, and is still active, with its headquarters now in a new hall on the corner of Main and Union Streets. During the years when Nantucket shipmasters were active in England, France, Holland, and Spain, their affiliation with the Masonic order forged an interesting international link. An apron of silk from China bearing the symbols of the order is still in existence on the island; it was made for a Nantucket captain in Canton about the time the Lodge Building was constructed.

In the year 1870, Captain David Thain decided to build a new home on the land adjoining the Lodge Building. Needing more room, he purchased one-half of the Lodge and tore it down. Thus, only the east section of the original building now stands, but fortunately, since it was restored, it presents a pleasant example of the entire Lodge design. Incidentally, the Thain house was completed during the lowest ebb of Nantucket's economic fortune, and it was grimly prophesized that this dwelling would be the last mansion built in the town. Ironically, this had an odd sequel, inasmuch as the Victorian home of Captain Thain was itself demolished in 1965, to allow space for a garden attached to the brick dwelling next door. It therefore did not reach its own century mark; the old Lodge Building, on the other hand, has not only survived, but continues in its second century to serve an important role in community life.

There is probably no single street in Nantucket which has as wide a range of maritime history as India Street. The name is derived from the number of shipmasters who lived there who made their living in the West India trade early in the eighteenth century. Whaling masters, coastwise skippers, merchant ship commanders, schooner captains—all were residents of this thoroughfare leading from North Liberty to Centre Street, living in homes ranging from small dwellings to mansions.

No. 19 India Street has an intriguing doorway. A flight of brownstone steps, on a brick foundation, is flanked by an iron railing and leads to a Federalist-style doorway with fanlight and sidelights. The porch is of the Greek Revival Period and has four slender pillars; the roof is embellished by a railed parapet. Zaccheus Hussey, a whaling merchant, built the two-story dwelling in 1807, with its brick side walls and high brick basement providing a contrast to its fellows. Captain Joseph Winslow purchased the house in 1863, following his retirement from a whaling master's career. His last command had been the bark *Amy,* one of the last of the Nantucket whaleships, which arrived home in 1870.

Captain Winslow began his seafaring life at an early age, rising steadily in the various grades until he received command of the old ship *Constitution* in 1852. Upon his return home the ship's owners, Charles G. and Henry Coffin, had the new ship *Constitution* built for him, and he sailed for the Pacific in 1857. It was on this voyage that Captain Winslow rescued Captain Guiseppe Oppisso and his eight-man crew, who had been adrift for nineteen days in an open boat after their ship had sunk in the South Atlantic.

Captain Winslow's wife and two daughters were on board during this voyage, and their remembrances of life on a whaleship became a vivid part of their lives, to be recounted to family and friends for years to come. Both enjoyed full, rich lives and spent their declining years in this fine old home on India Street.

When the U. S. Life Saving Service built the first Nantucket station at Surfside in 1874, it was Captain Joseph Winslow who was asked to be the first Keeper. In selecting his crew he had the

Joseph Winslow House. 19 India Street.

opportunity of choosing other ex-whalemen familiar with handling oars in open boats. After his service at Surfside, his retirement being mandatory by age limit, he continued an active life by taking fishing parties out in his catboat, and he became a popular figure along the waterfront.

Well along on Centre Street, at the corner of Gay Street, is the Joshua Coffin House, with the date of its construction, 1756, displayed over its doorway. The southeast portion of the house is the older, having been brought in from old Sherborn by Joshua Coffin. It was erected on land presented by his father-in-law, Peter Gardner, and the dwelling was later enlarged. In 1838 Captain Henry F. Coffin, grandson of the original owner, acquired the house, and today one of his descendants still owns it.

Captain Henry F. Coffin was an outstanding Nantucket shipmaster. He first went to sea on the whaleship *Ploughboy*, at the age of thirteen. On this voyage, during an attack on a sperm whale in the Pacific Ocean, the frail whaleboat in which young Coffin was a crew member was crushed by the whale. With his companions he clung to the wreckage during the night. Fortunately, the next morning the ship sighted and rescued them. The young whaleman bore the scar of a deep leg wound the rest of his life to remind him of the fearful episode. He later went into the merchant marine, and during the Civil War was an Acting Master in the U. S. Navy.

52 Centre Street is a fine old dwelling. There is a stalwart look about the entrance: the front steps leading to a square, balustered porch; the sidelights with louvered shutters; the well-proportioned door with two lights at the top, brass latch, and knocker; the pilasters which frame the doorway. A special feature of the house is a secret room carefully concealed within the chimney cluster, which can be reached from the attic through a trap door. In the days when privateers were lurking around New England shores many seaport families had secret hiding places for their silverware and valuables. Another feature: written in chalk on the rafters of the wide attic are names of Nantucket whaleships—*Lima,* 1826; *Ploughboy,* 1927; *Rose,* 1829; *Swift;*

Joshua Coffin House. 52 Centre Street.

and *Loper*. These were all famed in the history of Nantucket whaling.

Church Lane leads from Academy Lane to the Old North Vestry, the oak-beamed meeting house built in 1725 well to the west of its present site and later moved to Beacon Hill. Almost three-quarters of a century later (1834) it was again moved, this time to the rear of the new Congregational Church, which had been erected for a growing parish. The Academy was a private school; it stood on land south of the church, and gave its name to the entire area.

At the end of the lane stands a large dwelling with a distinctive front entrance portico. Erected in 1803 by Captain Reuben R. Bunker, it was remodeled two decades later into a fine example of the Federalist Period. The front is clapboarded; the sides were shingled. Twelve- over twelve-pane sashes add to the well-proportioned facade, and the roof walk commands a handsome view. The front entrance is particularly attractive, with an arched portico, a pair of graceful colonnettes, and a handsomely carved and detailed entablature. The steps provide a gradual ascent to the porch and front door, which has a fanlight that adds an excellent touch.

Captain Reuben R. Bunker made his career in the merchant service rather than in whaling. One of his successful commands was the ship *Logan* of New Bedford. Between the end of the Revolution and the War of 1812 the port of New Bedford engaged in lucrative European trade, with vessels sailing to Spain, Holland, and England and to Russian ports in the Baltic. From this "carrying trade" the New Bedford merchants derived considerable profit; it proved an excellent adjunct to their growing whaling business. And many Nantucket shipmasters were employed by the Bedford merchants, such as Captain Jared Gardner, Captain Andrew Pinkham, and Captain Reuben R. Bunker. The chinaware and other articles brought home by these merchant skippers are still the proud possessions of their descendants.

The Bunker mansion has had the good fortune to have had owners who continued to preserve its architectural features. Situated in an area where it has a certain privacy, the charm of this shipmaster's dwelling has been retained to a marked degree.

Reuben Bunker House. Church Lane.

Just past the wide entranceway to the North Congregational Church is the house built in 1796 by Captain Coffin Whippey, one of the Nantucket whaling masters who had gone to England and France after the Revolutionary War to take out whaleships from both England and France. It is now the Congregational Church parsonage. Though the house was originally of a lean-to design, the rear roof was raised to a high basement level by nineteenth-century owners.

Next door, 66 Centre Street, now known as Anchor Inn, was built in 1806 by Captain Archaelus Hammond—a man who made international whaling history. Returning to his island home after a quarter of a century spent in British and French whaleships, Captain Hammond enjoyed a well-earned retirement in his two and a half-story house. The pilastered doorway, with lights as a transom, the double-flight steps, six- over six-paned sashes, and shingled side walls give the house a shipshape appearance indeed.

As one of the many Nantucket whalemen going to London shortly after the Revolution, Captain Hammond advanced in rank to become first mate of the new British whaleship *Emilia*. Sailing from London in August, 1788, under Captain Shields, the ship reached the Pacific early in 1789; it was the first whaleship to round Cape Horn. Archaelus Hammond was the first man to harpoon a sperm whale in this great ocean, the feat being duly recorded in a letter by one of the Enderby firm, her owners. Later Hammond became master of the Rotch whaleship *Cyrus*, out of Dunkirk, France, but unfortunately was captured by the British. Upon his release he went back to Dunkirk to assume command of another whaler.

It is of interest to note that between the Whippey and Hammond dwellings was a small general store, with a "back room" that was usually frequented by retired whaling masters. Many of these mariners had been employed at one time or another on British whaleships and so the gathering became known as the "London Club." There was perhaps no other New England seaport with as unique and as colorful a membership as the London Club of Nantucket.

Archaelus Hammond House. 66 Centre Street.

Small houses have had as much a share in Nantucket's history as the larger and more pretentious mansions. Furthermore, they have a more intimate and homey quality than their bigger fellows. No. 8 Academy Lane serves to illustrate these facts. Built around 1820 for Captain Alexander D. Bunker, this one and three-quarter-story house, with its clapboard front and shingled sides, sits modestly on the very edge of the road surface. The doorway is well designed, with pilasters, a glass transom, and louvered screen doors. A series of carved pieces—modillions—provide attractive decorative touches over the door under the cornice and along the facade under the eaves. They give an extra flourish to the simple lines of the dwelling.

Captain Alexander Bunker was a successful and highly respected whaling master. In 1817, after serving his apprenticeship before the mast, he became master of the famous ship *Brothers*. He made a fine voyage of a little over two years' duration and was rewarded with the command of the new whaleship *Ontario*. After two excellent voyages in the *Ontario* he took out the *Zone* and brought back some 2,614 barrels of sperm oil after a voyage of two years, three months. On his next voyage, in the ship *Clarkson,* he returned with nearly three thousand barrels; this time he cruised the Pacific for three years and nine months. His last voyage was in the ship *Panama,* from 1836 to 1839. He then retired from the sea after twenty-five years as an active whaler. Yet, another experience awaited him. When the U.S. government erected a lighthouse on Sankaty Head in 1850, Captain Bunker was appointed the first Keeper.

One may well imagine this modest dwelling as the home of this hearty veteran of the sea. There is a subtle quality about it —and a blending of character and wholesomeness. Both were certainly characteristic of Captain Alexander Downes Bunker.

One of the best examples of a full two-story house, front and rear, may be found at the corner of North Water Street and Sea Street. It was built in 1795 for Robert Brayton and miraculously escaped the flames of the Great Fire of 1846, being protected by

William Watson House. 15 North Water Street.

the brick house of Aaron Mitchell, which stood on the opposite corner and was itself gutted.

No. 15 North Water Street is built on a stone foundation and has the usual features of its period—a large central chimney, a four-bayed facade, and twelve- over twelve-paned windows. Its generous proportions give it a "four-square" look, and the fact that its doorway and frame are of the later Greek Revival Period adds a new dimension of charm.

In this dwelling, on January 19, 1834, a son was born to William and Mary (Macy) Watson and was named William Watson, Jr. His mother, a daughter of Peleg and Sarah (Wendell) Macy, was a woman of marked intellectual vigor and she became his first teacher. He became a pupil of the Coffin School and, upon graduation, attended the State Normal School at Bridgewater, Massachusetts. From his earliest years he showed an aptitude and interest in mathematics and, upon completing his Normal School course, he became a teacher in the sciences for two years. In 1855 he entered the Lawrence Scientific School at Harvard. Two years later he won one of the highly competitive Boyden Prizes. That same year he graduated summa cum laude with a B.S. degree in Engineering; the following year, while serving as an instructor in calculus at the Scientific School, he received a second degree.

After two years of study in Paris and France, his studies and research led him through Europe and, upon completing a course at the University at Jena, he received a Ph.D. Returning to the United States, he became intimately associated with Professor William B. Rogers, who was then planning to launch a new university of technology. When the Massachusetts Institute of Technology was founded in 1865, Dr. Watson became the first Professor in Mechanical Engineering at the Institute. His subsequent career found him being awarded one honor after another. He was elected a Fellow of the American Arts and Sciences, was appointed a U. S. Commissioner at the Vienna Exposition of 1873, and represented the American Society of Civil Engineers at the Paris Exposition in 1878. He was the author of many articles published in scientific journals and was elected to membership in

Alexander D. Bunker House. 8 Academy Lane.

several engineering and science organizations both in this country and in Europe.

He never forgot his Coffin School years. In the early years of the school's program of instruction in manual training for boys, he presented to the trustees four lathes and a full set of woodworking tools for the school's use.

In his busy life he found few opportunities to visit his island birthplace, but whenever he did come here he sought out young scholars and encouraged them to continue their studies in higher fields of education. His career was one to inspire many a Nantucket youth.

In contrast to the part in history shared by this fine old house is an incident related to the Civil War. One of the Nantucket heroes of that war was Lieutenant Leander F. Alley. A young whaleman just home from sea, Alley joined the Twentieth Massachusetts Regiment and distinguished himself in several battles, eventually being promoted to lieutenant. While leading his men up Marye's Heights during the Battle of Fredericksburg, Lieutenant Alley was killed. His body was brought home by a contingent of his fellow islanders in the regiment. In the first military funeral ever held on Nantucket, the body of Lieutenant Alley was carried from this house and brought to the Prospect Hill Cemetery for interment.

Thus, this dignified doorway has witnessed both triumph and tragedy, just as have many other Nantucket homes.

On the crown of Orange Street's hill stands a dwelling which is of two ages and periods. No. 28 Orange Street has a particularly graceful doorway, with a Doric portico featuring fluted columns and parapet. The older section was built in 1755 for Doctor Benjamin Tupper, a man of considerable controversy during the Revolutionary War. It was Tupper who entertained that famous French visitor to Nantucket—De Crevecoeur—in 1773, and whose drawing of the island was printed in the classic *Letters from an American Farmer,* that delightful book which contains such excellent descriptions of both Nantucket and Martha's Vineyard.

Benjamin Tupper House. 28 Orange Street.

The old house was relocated at the rear of the present larger mansion, which was built in 1833 by Charles Bunker and is of the Greek Revival Period in style. A two-story dwelling, with clapboards, large end chimneys, and a five-bayed facade, it has a quiet elegance as it rises from its high basement. Its cupola and parapet give it added style, and the handsome doorway brings to it considerable charm.

Among its various owners over the years was Everett U. Crosby, a man who, as an adopted islander, devoted many years to advancing the unique appeal of Nantucket; his writings did much to focus attention on the need for preserving its remarkable architectural heritage. At present, a descendant of the Mitchell family is the proud owner of 28 Orange Street.

'SCONSET: "The Patchwork Village."

On the southeast shore of Nantucket is the village of Siasconset, always called 'Sconset. It was originally a hamlet for fishermen, who built their tiny shelters for use in the seasons when the cod and halibut were running. Constructed in a variety of unusual styles, these tiny dwellings gave to the place the name of "The Patchwork Village." With the emergence, however, of 'Sconset as a summer resort in the last decades of the nineteenth century, these miniature cottages became favorite homes; with their odd additions and appendages they gave the village a unique charm. One enterprising man built replicas in another section of the area and these are often confused with the originals.

Many of 'Sconset's old structures are of eighteenth-century origin; among these is Nauticon Lodge, to which one writer attributed an even earlier age than the date affixed over its doorway—1734. Henry Chandlee Foreman, in his excellent book on 'Sconset, describes the "hanging loft" and other architectural features which mark the evolution of this tiny dwelling. Among its early owners were Obed Coffin, Jonathan Colesworthy, and Captain Edward Joy. The latter had commanded the whaleships *Lydia* and *Constitution,* and one may visualize his enjoyment of this

Nauticon Lodge. 'Sconset.

tiny domain upon retirement from the sea. The little door leads to an interior which has rooms built like staterooms—with narrow doorways—and a single large room, which was characterized by Foreman as "hardly large enough to contain a small family seated."

As one enters the village, a white, clapboarded dwelling with the name "Rosemary" over the door attracts the eye. For many years it was the summer home of George Fawcett and his wife Percy Haswell Fawcett, two outstanding members of the American theatre. When 'Sconset became the favored vacation spot for theatre folk, particularly those of the New York stage, the village became widely known as the "Actors' Colony," and such famous stage folk as Joseph Jefferson, William H. Thompson, DeWolf Hopper, Digby Bell, Frank Gilmore, Isabel Irving, and Robert Hilliard made their summer homes here. No more beloved people in the days of 'Sconset's theatrical heyday could be found than George Fawcett and Percy Haswell. From the days when their own Shakespearean Company headed the bill at Albaugh's Theatre in Baltimore to the golden era of the "Silent Movies," this delightful couple enjoyed a successful joint career.

One of the plays in which Percy Haswell played a leading role was called *Rosemary*. About the same time they purchased their 'Sconset home and they promptly named it after the play. Through its front doorway has passed many a famous stage celebrity—Mrs. G.H. Gilbert, one of the great comediennes with Augustine Daly's celebrated Repertory Company; Vincent Serrano and Harry Woodruff, leading men both on and off the stage; and Lillian Russell, who, after her marriage to Alexander Moore, visited the little village her theatrical contemporaries had adopted.

"Rosemary" is now owned by the daughter of Mr. and Mrs. Fawcett—Mrs. Margaret Fawcett Barnes—whose booklet " 'Sconset Heyday" is a delightful reminiscence of 'Sconset and the Actors' Colony in the early 1900's.

"Rosemary" in 'Sconset.

"The Corners" in 'Sconset.

In the center of the village is an ancient community pump gracing a well dug in 1776. Serving as a bulwark of the northern line of "Pump Square" is "The Corners," also known as "Meeresheim," a cottage with some remarkable architectural features, one being a sharply angled addition known as a "flounder wing." It was owned by Shubael Barnard in 1814, and each subsequent owner appears to have added a bit "here and there," so that now, with its split-gable end, it has become a favorite subject for artists.

The photograph brings out the entranceway on its south side, with trumpet vine and hollyhock gracing the Dutch door, with sunlight clearly bringing out its narrow window frame and small-paned sash—all so typical of the unique habitations which make up the honorable and ancient village of " 'Sconset by the Sea."

Return to Nantucket-Town.

Fair Street, laid out in 1717, has its proper share of notable dwellings, which range over two centuries. No. 40 Fair Street was built in 1827-28 by Captain Seth Pinkham, who was born directly across the way. Built in the typical Nantucket style, the two and a half-story house is on a brick foundation, and has a four-bayed facade. A short flight of steps with railed porch leads to the solid front door with a four-paned transom. Slender pilasters frame the door and support a "shelf" over the entrance.

After serving the usual apprenticeship as a young whaleman, Seth Pinkham went out as mate on the *Golden Farmer,* under Captain George Swain, II. The ship escaped the British blockade during the War of 1812, and Pinkham caught the attention of its owners, who gave him command of the ship *Dauphin* in 1815, in which vessel he made two good voyages. In 1820 he was master of the new ship *Galen* and returned in 1823 with a full cargo. It was with the proceeds from this voyage that he retired from whaling, and was later elected a representative from Nantucket to the State Legislature.

The panic of 1837 brought reverses to Captain Pinkham's financial condition, and he decided to undertake another whaling voyage. So in 1840 he went out in command of the ship *Henry Astor.* He never returned alive, for he was stricken at sea and died at Pernanbuco on the passage home. His body was brought back to Nantucket in a cask of pickle, to be interred in the family plot. It was a sad ending for a man whose courage was unquestioned. Both in his career and in his letters, Captain Pinkham was a scholar as well as a mariner. His biography, *Through the Hawse Hole,* written by his great-grandaughter, the distinguished writer Florence Bennett Anderson, is a fine study of a remarkable Nantucketer.

During his last voyage, Captain Pinkham wrote a thoughtful letter to his friend Barker Burnell, who was then representing Nantucket in the National Congress in Washington, urging him to work for legislation that would bring more naval protection for the American whalers in the Pacific as well as government sponsorship of expeditions to more properly chart the islands and waters of that great ocean.

Despite his death "homeward bound," Captain Pinkham sent the *Henry Astor* back to Nantucket with a full cargo, thus insuring for his family the financial security he had been determined to win.

At the foot of Main Street's cobbled square there is the three-story red brick building known as the Pacific Club; it has been a cornerstone in Nantucket history for two centuries. Built in 1772 by William Rotch, Sr., head of the whaling firm of William Rotch & Sons, this fine old structure served as that firm's counting house as well as the first Custom House for Nantucket Port in 1789. The Rotch firm, early in the spring of 1773, loaded the brigs *Beaver* and *Dartmouth* with whale oil and the ships sailed to London. On their return they carried cargoes of tea consigned to certain Boston merchants by the British East India Company, and thus became two of the three vessels involved in the famous Boston Tea Party.

William Rotch had another ship which made history—the *Bedford.* Dispatched to London with a cargo of Nantucket whale oil, the *Bedford* arrived at London in February, 1783 (before the Treaty of Paris was signed), and Captain William Mooers

Seth Pinkham House. 40 Fair Street.

hoisted for the first time in any British port the flag of the new nation, the United States of America.

It was not until a decade after the Rotch firm was transferred to New Bedford that William Rotch sold the building to a contemporary, Gideon Gardner, and it became headquarters for the Union Marine Insurance Company. With the resurgence of the island's whaling prosperity in the first decades of the nineteenth century, this building, with its Custom House and insurance firm, was one of the most important centers in the town. But just before the outbreak of the Civil War and the accompanying decline of Nantucket's whaling business, the insurance firm ended its affairs, and in 1861 the brick structure was sold to a group of retired shipmasters, who formed the Pacific Club—an organization which still functions, though the last of the square-rigger captains has long since passed away.

When the U.S. Weather Bureau was established in Nantucket in 1886, the Pacific Club became its headquarters for the next twenty years. Then, in 1913, the first District Court on Nantucket established a courtroom on the third floor, which continued until 1964. The Nantucket Chamber of Commerce now has an office on the second floor and a legal firm has had quarters here for over three decades.

The front entrance of the Pacific Club has remained unchanged since the time the building was restored after the Great Fire of 1846. Through this portal the venerable whaling masters would pass for their daily visits; seated around the big stove, they would talk, keeping a watchful eye on the activities of Main Street. Many a tale of a voyage was recounted here, as well as tales of the sea, of ships and men and whales. One day a few survivors of the original club noticed the tall elm that stood in front of the building showed obvious evidence of the toll of age. It had withstood the ravages of time, just as they too had lived, exposed to the elements, and they recognized the inevitable. But whereas the elm was replaced, when they vanished from the scene there could be no replacements.

As a symbol of this race of mariners and of the times in which they lived and ventured on voyages of years, the Pacific Club stands as a fitting and enduring monument.

Pacific Club. Main Street.

Shortly after returning from his last whaling voyage—as master of the newly built ship *Nantucket* (constructed on Brant Point)—Captain David N. Edwards had the Greek Revival-style mansion at 53 Centre Street built for his family and himself. It is one of the few dwellings in the town with a side porch entrance. The doorway is graced with an Ionic portico and a well-proportioned railed porch, with steps ascending on both sides.

When Captain Edwards moved into his new home in 1841 he had just retired from a whaling master's life of a quarter century of voyaging. He first went to sea as a boy, advanced steadily in command through the ship, and became a captain in 1825, when he was given command of the *Paragon.* After two good voyages in her he took out the ships *Harvest* and *Montano,* in which he continued his success. In 1837 he accepted command of the new ship *Nantucket,* built at Brant Point. At the end of this Pacific Ocean voyage, in which he took two thousand barrels of sperm oil, he decided to retire.

In his handsome new mansion on Centre Street he enjoyed forty-five years of retirement. He was active in community affairs and assumed the post of Senior Deacon in the North Congregational Church, where he was a valuable "pillar of the church" throughout the years. From the vantage point of his rooftop cupola, he often watched the harbor shipping that was marking the decline of the great industry in which he had been a success. He died at the age of eighty-four, after a bad fall he had while overseeing the shingling of his roof by carpenters. However, until hours before his passing, he maintained his reputation for being an active man.

When William Coffin had his new house built in 1818 at 18 Union Street he was already a successful man in several fields of endeavor. Over two decades before he had been appointed by President Washington as Nantucket's first Postmaster. Other activities included conducting a barber shop and fashioning wigs; investing in whaleships; serving as secretary for the Marine Insurance Company; and negotiating for real estate. He was also prominent as a director of the first Nantucket Bank.

David Edwards House. 53 Centre Street.

It was the mysterious robbery of this bank in June, 1795 (only a few weeks after it opened its doors), which literally divided the town into two factions—one side accusing some of the bank's directors, including William Coffin, of having planned the robbery, the other defending the accused. The controversy was bitter, continuing even after the courts had exonerated William Coffin and his associates. Nearly twenty years later a criminal held in a New York prison made a statement in which three professional thieves were identified as the actual robbers; they allegedly came to Nantucket in a sloop and carried out the crime. Using these facts and other collected details, William Coffin and a fellow bank director, Albert Gardner, published a pamphlet revealing the full story. As an interesting sequel, when the bank was finally dissolved in 1817 William Coffin had the brick front steps and the railing removed and re-erected as his own front entrance at 18 Union Street.

William Coffin's daughter, Martha, married a young Boston journalist named Samuel Haynes Jenks, who in 1821 became the editor of the first successful Nantucket newspaper, *The Inquirer.* Later he founded another paper, *The Warder;* it was published down the lane now called Coffin Street. The large white house on the corner opposite the Coffin House was built in 1830 for Samuel and Martha Jenks. When the Great Fire of 1846 burned out the two other newspaper offices—those of *The Inquirer* and *The Mirror*—Jenks offered his own press for their printings.

When Admiral Sir Isaac Coffin, of the British Navy, made his first visit to Nantucket, he was a guest at 18 Union Street. Here he announced his desire to erect a fitting monument to Tristram Coffin, the Nantucket ancestor of all the Coffins in America, and it was William Coffin and Samuel H. Jenks who convinced the doughty old admiral that a school might serve as the most fitting memorial. The next year (1827) the Coffin School was founded, and William Coffin became the first President of the Board of Trustees. In 1852, when the present brick Coffin School was erected on Winter Street, the portraits of both Admiral Sir Isaac Coffin and William Coffin were hung in the handsome main room of the structure.

William Coffin House. 18 Union Street.

The Oldest House. Sunset Hill.

That venerable dwelling on Sunset Hill known as the Coffin House was built in 1686 for the newlyweds Joshua Coffin, grandson of Tristram Coffin, and Mary Gardner, daughter of Captain John Gardner. The wedding serves as a fitting sequel to that earlier chapter in the island's history in which Tristram Coffin and John Gardner engaged in a legal and political battle for control of the basic policy of Nantucket life: should the island be controlled by the old English tenant farmer system or should it be a place for the individual freedom of its inhabitants in ownership of the land. Gardner's party for democracy won the day.

While the "Oldest House," as it is now known, was for years called the "Horseshoe House"—because of the inverted horseshoe design in the top of the brick chimney—and known as the "Coffin House" as well, it actually should be called the Coffin-Paddack House. Joshua and Mary Coffin lived little more than twenty years in the dwelling; it was sold in 1708 to the Paddack family, who owned it for over a century. Here was born a number of the most famous of Nantucket's whaling masters of the eighteenth century, and here grandsons named West listened to stories of sea adventures that inspired many accomplishments of their own as shipmasters.

George Turner bought the house from the Paddacks in 1804; his children were the last to be born in the old structure. In 1881, when the Coffin family reunion was held on the island, Tristram Coffin, of Poughkeepsie, New York, found the house in ruins and purchased it, thus saving it from a certain end. He transferred ownership to the Nantucket Historical Association in 1924, and three years later it was restored under the guidance of Sumner Appleton, of the Society for the Preservation of New England Antiquities, and Alfred Shurrocks, a resident architect. Today it is open each season to the public and is one of the most popular of the association's exhibit buildings.

A story and half high, of the lean-to design, with a long sloping roof to the rear and the front facing the south, with its huge central chimney, wide fireplaces, exposed structural beams, and general air of olden times, Nantucket's Oldest House is a simple but dramatic monument to the families of the first settlers on the island.

In 1811, Joseph Samson, an observant visitor, wrote an article on Nantucket for the *Portfolio* of Philadelphia, in which he described India Street as having been so named because of "the number of residents who live in ease and affluence thereon." A little more research on the part of the writer would have revealed that there were a number of shipmasters living along India Street who made excellent voyages to both the West and East Indies. Most of the dwellings were built from money directly connected with marine trade both to the West Indies and the Far East.

At No. 20 India Street, Captain Robert Inott moved in with his bride Judith Folger, daughter of Paul Folger, soon after their marriage in 1782. The doorway is one of the most attractive of the period houses on the street, being of the Greek Revival style. It dates much later than the house itself, but with its well-shaped stoop and the touch of ornateness in its framing, it provides a handsome entrance.

Captain Inott's father, Joseph, was killed by a whale when Robert was only three years old, and his mother, Eliza (Gardner) Inott, never remarried. After the usual apprenticeship as a whaleman Robert took command of the old ship *Samuel* for a voyage to the Pacific. He learned of the new sealing grounds at the South Shetlands and sailed into the Antarctic seas in 1821. He was only moderately successful, and on the way home he was forced into Rio de Janeiro, where the ship was condemned and the oil shipped home. He then took a merchantman on a voyage for logwood to Honduras. Here he contracted yellow fever and died at the age of sixty-two.

His life was one of hardships and missed opportunities. One of the Nantucket men who knew him once wrote that when the embryo sail-steamship *Savannah* was built in New York in 1817, Captain Inott took her out—presumably on a trial run. It was Captain Moses Rogers who commanded the vessel on her pioneer steam-sail voyage from Savannah to Liverpool in 1819. The questions arise: Was Captain Inott offered the command? And did he decide against the venture? Despite the initial effort in this

Robert Inott House. 20 India Street.

unprecedented attempt and despite the historic overtones, the *Savannah*'s voyage was not a financial success. This possibility may have entered Captain Inott's mind if he had been offered the command.

The tragic overtones of his family's sea history appears evident in the deaths of Captain Inott's three sons. Robert, Jr., was drowned at the age of two when he fell off one of the wharves; Alexander was lost at sea shortly after his marriage ot Eliza Walcott; and Joseph died aboard a whaleship en route to Nantucket from Dunkirk.

The heavy oaken door, which swings on wide iron hinges and is reinforced with iron straps bolted to the inner side, boasts a lock so strong that it is impossible to open without the massive key. This is the entrance to the "Old Gaol" on Nantucket, the oldest of its kind in New England. Built after the style of a log cabin, it has logs for walls and ceilings and floors that have been bolted together with iron "drifts." Oak planks cover the interior walls and floors of the four cells, there being two on each floor of the two-story building. One of the lower cells is sheathed with iron straps—for "solitary confinement." The main doorway leads to the lower cells and an outside staircase provides a means of access to the upper cells, which have a smaller outside entrance door. The west cells, both upper and lower, have fireplaces, and each of the four cells has two small heavily barred windows.

Constructed in 1805 by John and Perez Jenkins, the extraordinary strength of Nantucket's ancient jail was planned so that an episode in the history of the first jail would not be repeated. Some experienced criminals had broken free from this earlier-built structure (which had been located in the center of the town) and had escaped in boats stolen from the wharves. The town's authorities vowed this would not be repeated.

But, while no one has ever escaped from the jail by forcing the doors or bending the bars of the windows, one youth, who was slight in size, surprised the jailer by forcing his way up through the fireplace and dislodging enough bricks to reach the roof, from where he slid down and escaped. New granite lintels,

The Old Jail. Vestal Street.

heavy bars in the flues, and smaller hearths have prevented any further incidents of a similar nature. But escapes have occurred —one man gained freedom by running away while exercising in the yard; another got away when his wife, noting the padlock to the outer door was not fastened, stole the jailer's key to the cell and passed it to her husband through the small aperture in the cell door. The man freed himself in the night, walked to the west end of the island, stole a dory, and rowed out into Nantucket Sound. The next day a schooner picked him up off Cross Rip and he went to New York in her. Several weeks later an acquaintance recognized him working on a wharf near the Fulton Fish Market and alerted the New York police; he was brought back to Nantucket to complete his sentence for breaking and entering and theft.

In the early nineteenth century, when the town had a thriving waterfront, the jail was well occupied—especially by brawling sailors who met in the several wharf taverns or "grog shops," as they were termed. Imprisonment for debt was common in those days, also. Others brought here were guilty of minor crimes—one man was sentenced to six months imprisonment for stealing a coat!

In 1854 the town had its House of Correction moved into town and placed next to the jail. Here many prisoners were allowed to furnish their rooms with their own possessions while serving a sentence. Probably the most famous of those unfortunate people who lived for months and even years in this structure was a black woman named Patience Cooper, who had killed a woman storekeeper named Phebe Fuller during an argument in the latter's store, maintained in the Fuller home on Silver Street. Patience Cooper at first vowed her innocence, but after five years as an inmate in the House of Correction she suddenly announced she would confess to the crime. Two years later, her health having deteriorated, she was pardoned and returned to her little home on lower Pleasant Street. During the time she was a prisoner she was permitted to "take in washing," and thus earned money for herself. Many of the townspeople brought family laundry to her, and she had numerous "visits" with friends—but only a few were intimate associates.

Toward the end of the nineteenth century the Old Jail became a curiosity and the number of people placed therein was few. Many humorous stories are still told about the inmates: one man, a shoemaker, was allowed to carry on his business there; a bank cashier who had misappropriated funds had his second-floor cell completely furnished with his own household rugs, chairs, bed, and bureaus during his two years' sentence; an older man, who enjoyed walking in the jail yard, sent a letter to the selectman protesting some broken boards in the high fence, stating that this permitted sheep to get into the enclosure and cause a nuisance; and one of the jailers saw to it that certain inmates were given permission to leave the premises for several hours on good days when the blueberry season was on, only insisting they be back in their cells by dark.

The Old Jail was used by the town until 1933, when a prisoner, arrested on a serious charge and awaiting trial, struck the jail keeper from behind as he brought in his supper and ran out into the darkness. The young man was able to escape from the island. Nearly five years later, due to a bit of detective work on the part of the Nantucket tax collector, a man held in a California prison was identified as the escapee; he was returned to Nantucket and received a heavy sentence.

Today, the Nantucket jail is an exhibit of the Nantucket Historical Association. The old door, with its grim story, serves as an entrance into a part of Nantucket's past which is a chilling reminder of when man's inhumanity to man was an accepted part of everyday life.

On the west corner of Milk Street and Quaker Road is a commodious dwelling with an interesting history. It was originally the boat-builder's shop of Hiram and Charles Folger, and stood some distance to the north on Quaker Road. In 1817 the Folgers sold the shop to George and Reuben Coffin, also builders of whaleboats as well as wheelwrights. It was known as the "Big Shop."

In the 1830's it became an evening meeting place for neighborhood residents as well as a warehouse for sales of candle boxes, wool—when the sheep were sheared—and codfish during the spring and fall seasons. The evening sessions attracted many residents of the west end of the town, and all manner of subjects were discussed by the gatherings, especially the affairs of the time relating to politics.

The militant abolitionists from the mainland, notably William Lloyd Garrison and Stephen Foster, often came to Nantucket to raise money for their cause, but the rabid criticism of the churches by Foster finally brought about refusal on the part of the islanders to honor his requests for the use of churches or public halls. The "Big Shop" was made available to Garrison and his party when they held meetings in 1841. It was during the first meeting here that a dramatic episode was enacted. Garrison was addressing the gathering when he noticed he had lost the attention of his listeners. On the platform with his group was a young black man named Frederick Douglass, an escaped slave from Virginia. Realizing the immediate necessity of regaining the crowd's attention, Garrison turned to Douglass and asked him to stand and tell of his experiences in the South and of his hazardous journey to freedom.

Momentarily embarrassed, the young man got to his feet and began to speak haltingly. When he saw the instantaneous sympathy in the faces of the gathering he took heart. It was his first public appearance, but before he had completed his address his natural ability asserted itself, and when he had finished the people were on their feet, according him a standing ovation. History has recorded how Frederick Douglass later became one of the leading figures in the antislavery cause, as well as one of the greatest orators and writers of his time.

The "Big Shop" closed its doors in 1848, when whaling was declining, and soon after was converted in part to a dwelling. It was moved to its present site in 1885, and remodeled as a complete dwelling house several years later. In 1946 it was purchased by Mr. and Mrs. James K. Glidden, of Nantucket, who, with extensive improvements, have turned the durable strong-timbered structure into a handsome and commodious family home.

"The Big Shop"—Glidden House. 35 Milk Street.

It should be noted that the houses of Nantucket divide the town's history equally between themselves, whether large, medium-sized, or small, so that together they represent the true story of Nantucket's rich maritime past. In the modest home at 31 Pine Street, in the late nineteenth and early twentieth centuries, lived Captain Henry Folger, a man of small stature and quiet disposition. He was the master of schooners bringing coal, wood, and grain to Nantucket from ports that ranged the coast from Norfolk to Eastport. Known for his excellent seamanship, he had a further reputation for never losing a vessel. He once remarked that his favorite schooner was the *Island City,* because, as he stated, "she never missed stays." Only those who have been on heavily loaded big schooners can appreciated this simple expression of a vessel's qualities when "coming about."

In his declining years he saw the schooner fleet dwindle to a single vessel, and he often commented on the changing atmosphere of the waterfront as the days of sail were ending. He was of a thrifty nature, and, at an age when most elderly men were content to rest, he was often seen trundling a wheelbarrow along the wharves and gathering pieces of wood for his stove—usually accompanied by his favorite companion, a large dog.

As so many times happens with men of seafaring experience, Captain Folger neither kept a diary nor left a written record of his coastal voyages. He was typical of the humble men who did not regard their lives as worthy of record, when so much of their work would have served as excellent examples of the quality of their quiet and obscure accomplishments.

One islander who, as a small boy, lived close by will not forget this modest schooner captain. In reply to a question, the latter would always answer with as much courtesy as he accorded an adult. His voice was marked by a clear resonance, vibrant and deep-toned. "Well," he would say, in reply to a question as to the advantages of a schooner in coastal waters as compared to a square-rigged vessel, "when you're caught on a lee shore, in a northerly, you have to claw your way out of trouble. Running close-hauled in a fore-'n'-aft vessel, you have a chance of getting

Henry Folger House. 31 Pine Street.

free." Using a pencil and a handkerchief, he would then demonstrate sail handling.

On another occasion, he was asked: "What did you find as your chief aid in navigating up and down the coast?" He replied quickly: "My anchor!" And in his explanation, the boy-neighbor received one of the finest lessons in seamanship (and also one of the earliest) he could ever learn.

In our own century this house has a claim to history—albeit it in a far different realm than the sea coast of Captain Folger.

Nantucket has long since been an attractive place for artists, writers, and musicians who find the island's atmosphere conducive to creative work. In the early 1940's the playwright Tennessee Williams spent several months in the first floor apartment at 31 Pine Street; it was there he wrote his famous drama *A Streetcar Named Desire.* Two decades earlier, another famous writer of plays, Eugene O'Neill, resided for two summers in an ancient house on Mill Street, where he worked on *Strange Interlude.* It is probable that *Mourning Becomes Electra* was also planned here, as the dramatic background of this seaport town had an instinctive appeal to this outstanding American playwright.

As a segment of our nation's history Nantucket has contributed its own unique part, and its preservation is important to the continuing story of our national heritage.

Corner India and Centre Streets, 1861. Built after the Great Fire of 1846.

Nantucket in 1881. Thirty-five years after the Great Fire of 1846 the newly built section of Nantucket blended so well with the old that only the memory remained.

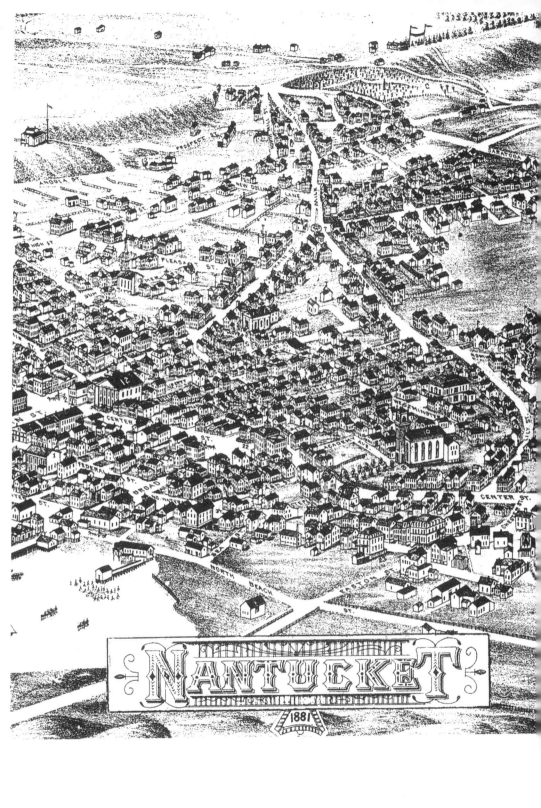

NANTUCKET

1881

Main Street Square after a snowstorm, February, 1930.

Vestal Street's west end has the same dwellings today which appeared in this photo taken in 1881.

INDEX

Folger, Charles, 135
Folger, Miss Gulielma, 14
Folger, Capt. Henry, 138-40
Folger, Henry C., 46
Folger, Henry Clay, 46-47
Folger, Hiram, 135
Folger, Capt. Isaiah, 60-62
Folger, James Athearn, 44, 46
Folger, John, 36
Folger, Judith, 130
Folger, Capt. Mayhew, 66-67
Folger, Paul, 130
Folger, Samuel, 44
Folger, Walter, Jr., 49
Folger's Coffee, 46
Foreman, Henry Chandlee, 114, 116
Fosdick, Benjamin, 21
Fosdick, Reuben, 21
Foster, Stephen, 136
Fuller, Phebe, 134

Galatin, 97
Galen, 119
Gardner, Albert, 126
Gardner, Arthur H., 60
Gardner, Crispus, 59
Gardner, Eliza, 130
Gardner, George, 32
Gardner, Gideon, 122
Gardner, Grace Brown, 60
Gardner, Grafton, 32
Gardner, Capt. Jared, 56, 104
Gardner, John, 129
Gardner, Lydia, 40-41, 59
Gardner, Margaret, 59
Gardner, Mary, 129
Gardner, Peter, 102
Gardner, Capt. William B., 60
Gardner, Rev. William E., 41
Garrison, William Lloyd, 136
George, 24
Gilbert, Mrs. G. H., 116
Gilmore, Frank, 116
Glidden, James K., 136
Glidden House, 136
Globe, 59
Golden Farmer, 119

Gold Rush (Calif.), 8, 44-46, 60, 74, 79
Great Point Lighthouse, 31, 32
Greyhound, 40
Griffin, Rev. Fr. Joseph M., 41, 50

Hadwen, family, 79
Hadwen, Anna Ray, 84
Hadwen, William, 74, 79-84
Hadwen-Satler House, 74-75, 79-84
Hallett, Reuben, 56
Hammond, Capt. Archaelus, 106
Harvest, 124
Haswell, Percy, 116
Hayscale Lane, 29, 32
Henry Astor, 119, 120
Hiller, Nancy, 44
Hilliard, Robert, 116
Hodges, Capt. Sylvester, 22
Hope, 40
Hopper, DeWolf, 116
"Horseshoe House," 129
House of Correction, 134
Hummock Pond, 34
Huntress, 90
Huron, 90
Hussey, Capt. Benjamin, 18
Hussey, Cyrus, 59
Hussey, Cyrus, the elder, 59
Hussey, Phoebe, 18
Hussey, Zaccheus, 100

India Street, 130; No. 19, 100; No. 20, 130
Inott, Alexander, 132
Inott, Eliza, 130
Inott, Joseph, 130, 132
Inott, Capt. Robert, 130-32
Inott, Robert, Jr., 132
Inquirer and Mirror, The, 28, 126
Irving, Isabel, 116
Island City, 138
Islander, 50

Jefferson, Joseph, 116
Jenkins, John and Perez, 132
Jenks, Martha, 126

Siasconset, *see* 'Sconset
Society of Friends, 34, 36, 41, 54, 68
Southern Whale Fishery, 7, 10, 16, 64
South Shetland Islands, 22, 90, 130
Spartan, 50
Starbuck, family, 75, 79, 84
Starbuck, Capt. Charles, 50
Starbuck, Christopher, 64
Starbuck, George, 62
Starbuck, Joseph, 62, 84-86
Starbuck, Levi, 29
Starbuck, Lydia, 16
Starbuck, Mary, 34, 36
Starbuck, Matthew, 62, 84-86
Starbuck, Molly, 50
Starbuck, Nathaniel, 34, 36
Starbuck, Thomas, 19
Starbuck, William, 19, 62
Stevens, William O., 49
Stewart, Colonel Robert, 14
Stewart, Robert W., 56
Story, Thomas, 34
Summer Street, No. 7, 41
Sunset Hill, 128
Surfside, 100-2
Swain, family, 79
Swain, Mary G., 79
Swain, Valentine, 77
Swain, Capt. William, 21-22
Swain II, Capt. George, 119
Swift, 103
Swift, family, 79
Swift, Henry, 86

Tarquin, 72-74
Telassar, 74
Thain, Capt. David, 99
Thompson, William H., 116
"Three Bricks," 62, 84-86
Three Brothers, 62, 75, 84
Trader's Lane, 38
Tropaz, 67
Tupper, Dr. Benjamin, 112
Turner, George, 129

Union Marine Insurance Co., 122

Union Street, No. 18, 124, 126
Unitarian Church, 86

Walcott, Benjamin, 38
Walcott, Eliza, 132
Walnut Lane, 92
Wannacomet Pond, 19
Warder, The, 126
War of 1812, 18, 21, 24, 54, 68, 119
Watson, Mary, 110
Watson, William, 110
Watson, William, Jr., 110-12
Wave, 97
Weather Bureau, U.S., 122
Webb, Charles Henry, 92-94
Webster, Daniel, 21
Wendell, Sarah, 110
Wesco Acre Lots, 16
West, family, 129
West, Paul, 18-19
West, Stephen, 66
Whaling, 7, 9, 16, 36, 44, 64, 72, 90, 106, 122
Whippey, Capt. Coffin, 106
William Rotch & Sons, 120-22
Williams, H. B., 56
Williams, Tennessee, 140
Wing Cher, 67, 68
Winslow, Capt. Joseph, 100-2
Woodruff, Harry, 116
Worth, Capt., 59
Worth, Ann Young, 24
Worth, Capt. Benjamin, 22-24
Worth, Capt. Charles, 24
Worth, Henry B., 56
Wright, George W., 79
Wyer, Catherine, 86
Wyer, Capt. Christopher, 86
Wyler, Capt. James, 50

Young, Ann, 24
Young, Martha, 75
Young Hero, 62

Zenas Coffin, 95
Zone, 108